Raspberry Pi 4

The New Updated Guide to Master the New Raspberry Pi 4 and Make, Build, or Hack a Variety of Amazing Projects

Sam O. Collins

Copyright © 2019 Sam O. Collins

All rights reserved. This book is copyright and no part of it may be reproduced, distributed, or transmitted in any form or by any means, including photocopying, recording, or other electronic or mechanical methods, without the prior written permission of the publisher, except in the case of brief quotations embodied in critical reviews and certain other noncommercial uses permitted by copyright law.

Printed in the United States of America

Copyright © 2019 Sam O. Collins

Contents

Introduction 1

Chapter 1: Setting up Your New Raspberry Pi 4 6

Chapter 2: Setting Up Your SD Card 14

    Formatting the SD Card 15

    Extracting NOOBs from the zip archive 17

Chapter 3: Connecting Your Raspberry Pi 19

    For Raspberry Pi 4 21

Chapter 4: Starting Up Your Raspberry Pi 4 24

    The First-Time Startup Using The NOOBS 24

    Finishing the Setup 25

Chapter 5: Raspberry Pi Desktop 28

    Keyboard and Mouse Settings 30

Chapter 6: Connecting To the Internet 32

    Setting up The Sound 33

    Installing Software 34

    Installing a Drawing Application Called Pinta 37

Chapter 7: Updating and Upgrading Raspbian 39

    Updating your Raspberry Pi 40

    Advanced Packaging Tool (APT) 43

    Upgrading from Jessie to Stretch 45

    Third-Party Solutions 46

    Mender 48

Chapter 8: How to Access Your Files 49

Chapter 9: Using the Terminal 55

Chapter 10: Configuring your Pi 58

Chapter 11: The Chromium Web Browser 63

Chapter 12: Programming With Scratch 66

    The Scratch 2 interface 67

    Scratch 3 68

GPIO extension 72

    Simple Electronics Extension 73

    Sense HAT Extension 74

    Looping the Loop 83

    Variables and Conditionals 85

    Counting From Zero 90

Chapter 13: Your first Scratch Project—Astronaut Reaction Timer .. 96

Chapter 14: Second Scratch Project—Synchronised Swimming 107

Chapter 15: Project 2: Archery Game 116

Chapter 16: Programming With Python 122

    Introducing the Thonny Python IDE 123

    Syntax error 126

Chapter 17: Your First Python Projects—Turtle Snowflakes 131

Chapter 18: Your Second Python Project—Scary Spot the Difference
.... 143

Chapter 19: Python Project 3– RPG Maze 153

Chapter 20: Physical Computing with Raspberry Pi 4 170

    Introduction to GPIO Header 170

    Reading Resistor Color Codes 178

Chapter 21: Your first Physical Computing Program: Hello, LED! 181

    LED Control in Scratch 185

    LED Control in Python 187

    Using a Breadboard 190

Chapter 22: Reading a Button 192

    Reading a Button in Scratch 193

    Reading A Button In Python 196

Chapter 23: Make Some Noise: Controlling a Buzzer 199

    Controlling A Buzzer In Scratch 200

    Controlling a buzzer in Python 201

Chapter 24: Scratch project: Traffic Lights 203

Chapter 25: Python project: Quick Reaction Game 209

Chapter 26: Physical Computing With Sense HAT 218

Chapter 27: Raspberry Pi 4 Projects— Creating a Portable Security Box on Raspberry Pi, 2, 3 and 4 225

    Creating A Portable Security Box 225

    The Installation of Kali on Raspberry Pi 229

    Installation of Hacking Tools 230

Chapter 28: Raspberry Pi 4 Projects—Setting up Raspberry Pi as a VPN Server 232

    How to find your Raspberry Pi 238

    Static IP 241

    Paranoia Level 243

    Getting Connected To Pi 244

    Access Granted 248

Chapter 29: Installing Full Windows 10 on Raspberry Pi 3 And 4 252

    Running Windows 10 IoT Core on Raspberry Pi 253

    Installing Windows 10 Iot Core on Raspberry Pi 255

    Preparation of your Raspberry Pi for IoT Core 257

Chapter 30: Troubleshooting 7 Tips 270

Introduction

Raspberry Pi is an ultra-small and affordable computer that costs less than most video games you could find around. With the Raspberry Pi 4, you can use it to build robots, learn coding, create wonderful projects, and create all kinds of weird stuff. Just like a computer would do, Raspberry Pi is able to do all the things you'd expect from a Personal Computer – meaning, you can browse everything from the internet and play games, watch movies and listen to music.

Raspberry Pi is even much more than a modern PC as it allows you to get into the heart of a computer. That is, you can easily use it to set up your own operating system, have wires and circuits connected directly to the pins on its board. The raspberry Pi was also built to teach young people how to easily program in languages like Python and scratch, as well as all the major programming languages that are available with the official operating system.

The Raspberry Pi has been upgraded and re-designed into Raspberry Pi 4 working faster than the previous version.

The Raspberry Pi 4 is a credit-card sized electronic board just like the one found in our personal computer but smaller in size when compared to the electronic board in computers.

Functions of the Raspberry Pi 4

- The Pi boards can be used as file servers, media centers, retro game consoles, network-level ad-blockers, and routers.
- They can be used in building phones, tablets, laptops, smart mirrors, and robots.
- The Pi boards are also useful for taking pictures on the edge of space.
- They are also useful for running experiments on the International Space station.
- Due to the fast speed of the Pi 4, it is also useful for decoding 4K video, deriving from faster storage through the USB 3.0 as well as faster network connections through the true Gigabit Ethernet.
- It supports the dual displays 4K output thereby can support two screens at once which is handy when users need more desktop space.

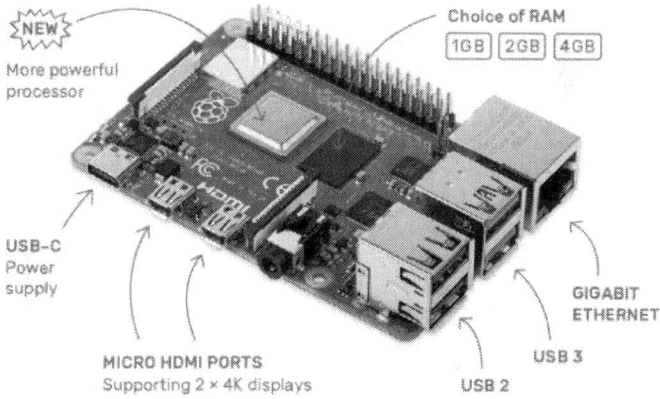

Dual Displays 4K Output

With the Raspberry 4, you can now get to run two monitors at a time using the 4k

New Desktop Computer

The Raspberry Pi 4 is now made up of a new complete desktop experience and now useful for getting documents edited, making use of tabs in browsing the web, working on different spreadsheets at once and efficient drafting of presentations.

Silent, Energy-Efficient

The Pi 4 is built with no fan in it and it is known to be efficient in terms of its energy using far less power when compared to other computers.

Networking

The Pi 4 is made up of Gigabit Ethernet as well as the Bluetooth and onboard wireless networking.

USB 3

They have been able to get the USB capacity upgraded in the Raspberry Pi 4. It now has the USB 2 ports as well as the two USB 3 ports that can be used in transferring data 10x faster.

RAM

They now have 1GB, 2GB or 4GB of RAM allowing users to choose whichever works for them.

Chapter 1: Setting up Your New Raspberry Pi 4

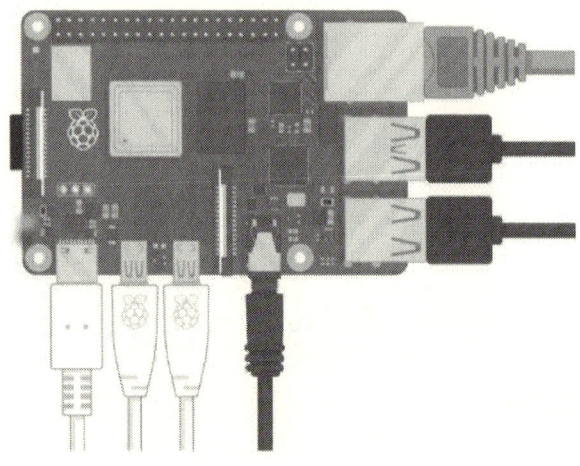

- There are different models of the Raspberry. The new Raspberry Pi 4 Model B is the choice of most users because of the faster speed and the ease of usage.
- They come with 1GB, 2GB or 4GB RAM. The 1GB of RAM version will be good enough for educational purposes as well as other projects while the 2GB of RAM will work fine when you decide to use the Pi 4 for tour desktop computer.
- Unlike the Raspberry Pi 4, the Raspberry Pi Zero and Zero are known to be smaller requiring less

power which makes them useful for carrying out portable projects like robotics.

- Projects can be easily started on the Raspberry Pi 4 and navigating to Pi Zero when there is a working prototype, one which the smaller Pi is useful for.

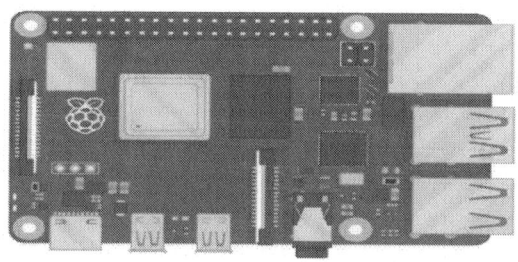

Power Supply

- It is to be noted that all Raspberry Pi models have a USB port similar to the ones available on mobile phones. We have the USB-C which is available in Raspberry Pi 4 and for the Raspberry Pi 3,2 and 1, there is a micro USB
- To connect to the power socket, a power that provides at least 3.0 amps will be needed for the Raspberry Pi 4.

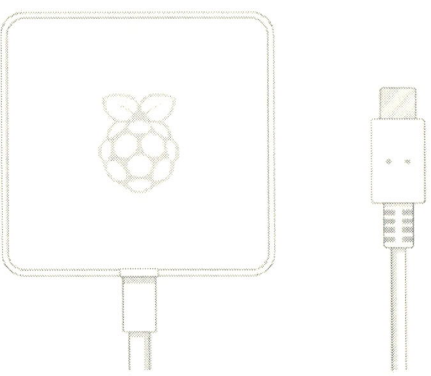

- It is also advisable to make use of your official universal power supply.

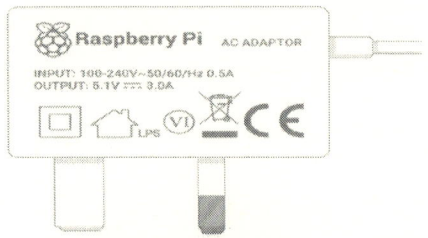

  ◦ At least 2.5 amps for Raspberry Pi 3

MicroSD card

- The SD card is used by the Raspberry Pi 4 for storing its files as well as the Raspbian operating system.

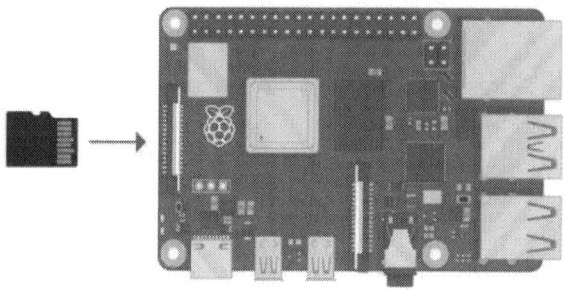

- The MicroSD must have a capacity of at least 8GB
- In most cases, the SD cards sold by sellers are already set up with Raspbian which makes them ready for use.

Keyboard and Mouse

- You will need a USB keyboard as well as a USB mouse to get started with the Raspberry Pi.
- A USB keyboard will be needed for the initial set up. Once you have the Pi set up, it will be ready to be used with the mouse and Bluetooth keyboard.

TV Or Computer Screen

- A screen, as well as a cable in linking the screen and the Pi, will be needed to view the Raspbian desktop environment.

- The computer monitor or TV can be used as a screen.
- The Pi can be used to play sounds as long as the screen is linked to have built-in speakers in it.

HDMI

- The Raspberry Pi is made up of HDMI output port which is compatible with the HDMI port found in the most modem, computer monitors as well as TVs. The DVI and VGA ports are also available in many computer monitors.
- The Pi 4 is made up of two micro HDMIs that enable you to connect two separate monitors.
- Either HDMI-to-HDMI cable or micro HDMI-to-HDMI cable with an HDMI-to-HDMI adapter is needed in connecting the Raspberry Pi 4 to a screen.

- There is a single full-size HDMI port that is useful in connecting the Raspberry Pi 1,2, and 3 to the screen by making use of an HDMI-to-HDMI cable.

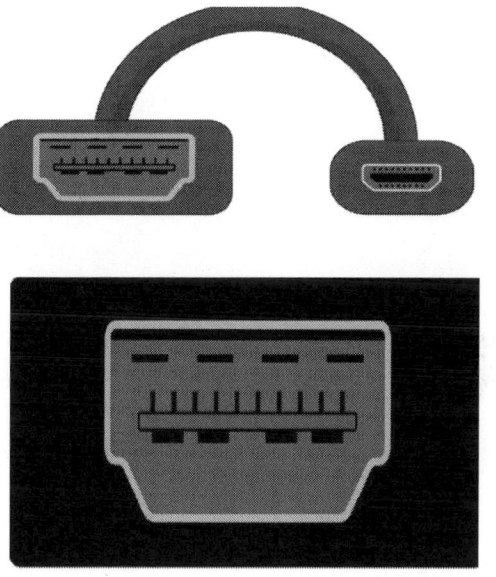

DVI

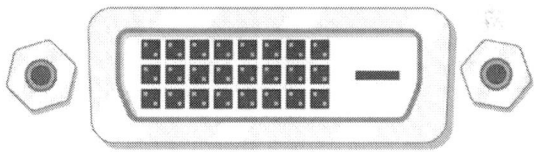

If the DVI port is available on your screen, the Pi can be connected with the use of HDMI-to-DVI cable.

VGA

In some cases, the only port available in screens is the VGA port so that when you are connecting the Pi to such a screen, you will need the use of an HDMI-to-VGA adapter.

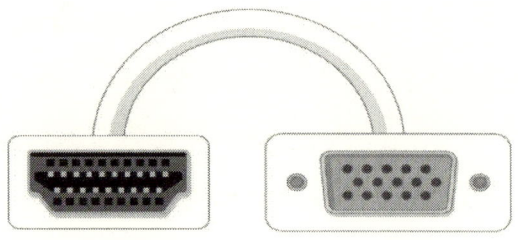

OPTIONAL EXTRAS

Case

It is optional to securely place your Raspberry Pi in a case to help in protecting your Pi.

Headphones or Speakers

The bigger Raspberry Pi models are made up of a standard audio port which is similar to the ones available on the smartphone or MP3 player.

This feature is not available in the Pi Zero/Zero W models. Though optional, you can get to connect your headphones or speakers which enable the Raspberry Pi to play sounds. The Raspberry Pi can also make use of speakers in playing sound if you have the built-in speakers on your screen.

Ethernet Cable

- The large Raspberry Pi is made up of a standard Ethernet port which is used for getting them connected to the internet. This feature is, however, missing in the Pi Zero/Zero W.
- The USB-to-Ethernet adaptor is needed in connecting Pi Zero to the internet.
- The Raspberry Pi 4, 3 and Pi Zero W can also be connected to the internet wirelessly.

Chapter 2: Setting Up Your SD Card

If your SD card is yet to have the Raspbian operating system or if you want to reset your Raspberry Pi 4, you can simply install the Raspbian yourself.

To do this, you will need a computer that contains an SD card port in it and luckily most desktop computers and laptops are known to have this.

Raspbian Operating system via NOOBS

- The use of the NOOBS is the easiest way of installing the Raspbian operating system on your SD card.
- Download NOOBS by visiting the Raspberry Pi downloads page

(To access the above link, get the ebook version free via matchbook if you are reading from the Paperback version of this book)

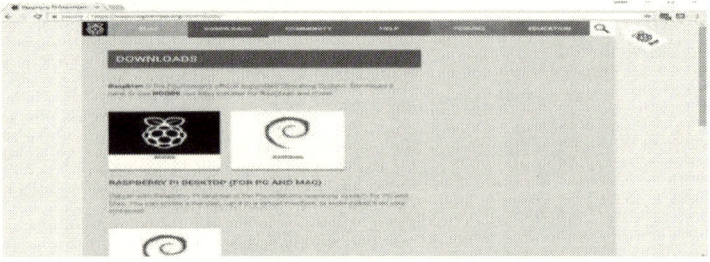

- Click on the box that links to the NOOBS files.

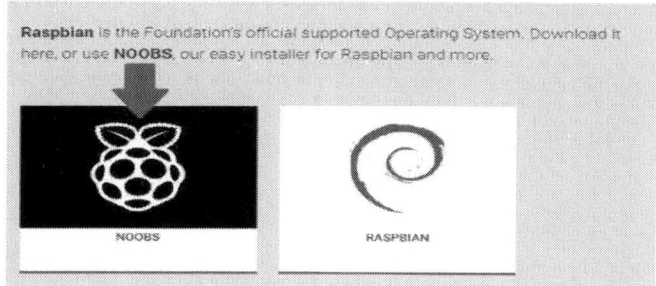

- Downloading the zip archive of the files is the simplest option and make sure you note where the archive is saved to have access to it quickly.

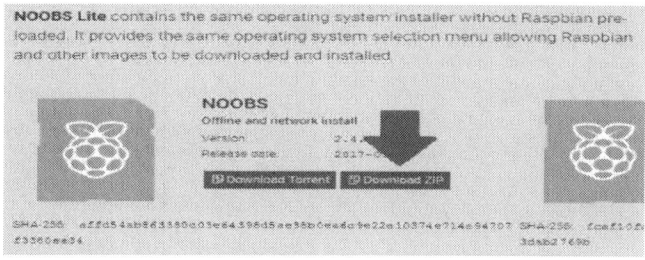

Formatting the SD Card

During the process of formatting the SD card, anything stored on the SD card will be overwritten which is why you will need to back up files on your SD card on which you want to install the Raspbian. This will save you from losing any of your files permanently.

i. Download SD Formatter for your Windows or Mac by visiting the SD Association's website.

ii. You will be prompted by on-screen instructions you will need to follow to get the software installed.

iii. Get the SD card installed into the laptop or computer's SD card slot.

iv. Go to the SD formatter and select your SD card.

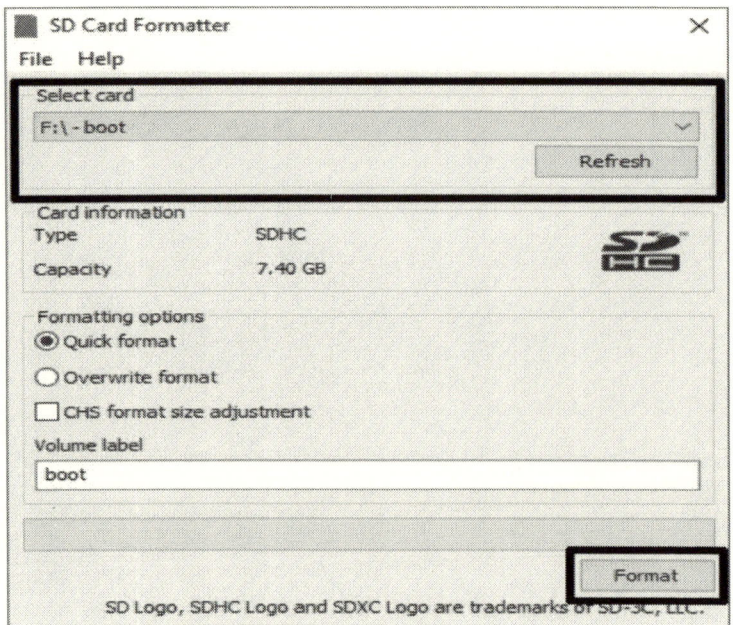

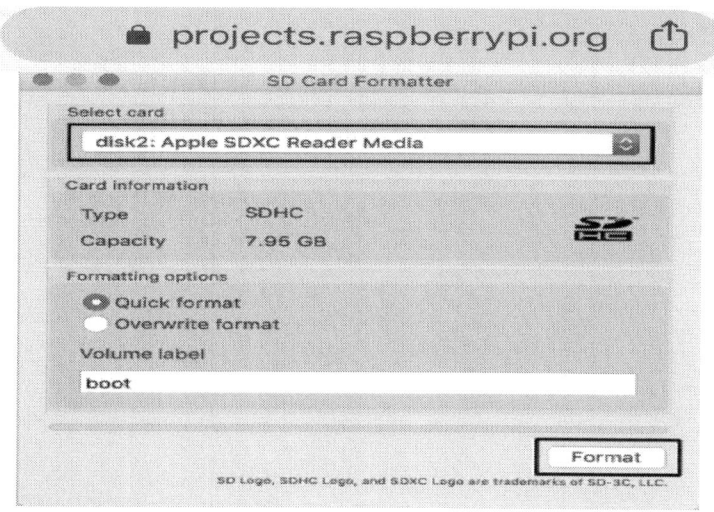

v. Format the card

Extracting NOOBs from the zip archive

To get files extracted from the NOOBS zip archive that was downloaded from the Raspberry Pi website, you will need to take the following steps:

i. Search for the downloaded archive which should be in your downloads folder by default.

ii. To extract the files, double-click the downloaded archive and store the Explorer/Finder window open.

Have the Files Copied

1. Open another Explorer/Finder and navigate to the SD card afterward.

2. It is advisable to position both windows side by side.

3. Go to the NOOBS folder and select all the files.

4. Drag them into the SD card window to copy them to the card.

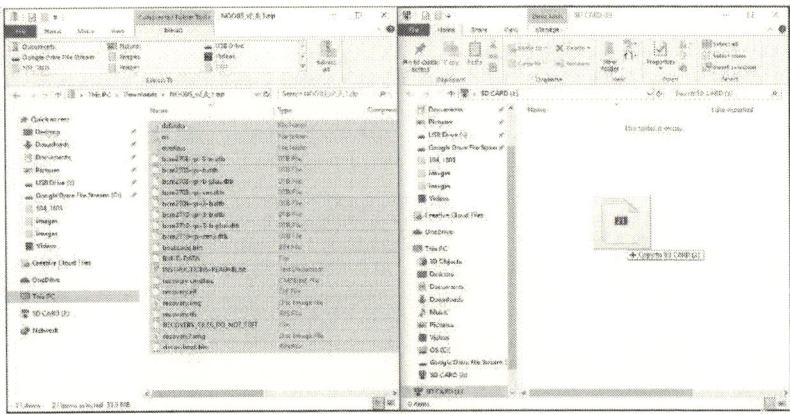

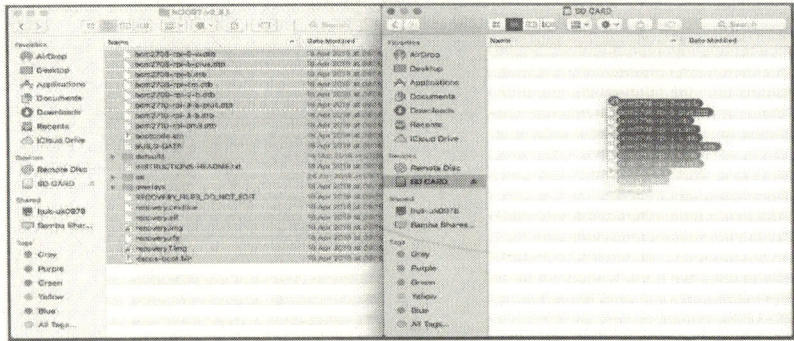

5. After copying all the files to the SD card, you can now have your SD card ejected.

Chapter 3: Connecting Your Raspberry Pi

To make optimal use of your Raspberry Pi, you will have to connect components you will need to it and most importantly it must be done in the right order to keep all your components safe.

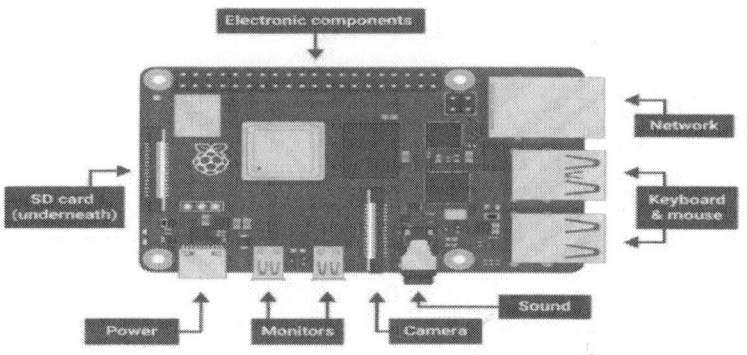

- Insert the SD card, which already has the Raspbian installed on it using the NOOBS, into the microSD card slot positioned on the underside of the Raspberry Pi.

- It is, however, important to note that most microSD cards come inside a larger adapter, so you can make use of the lip at the bottom in sliding your smaller card out.

- Search for the USB connector of your mouse's cable and have the mouse connected to a USB port on the Raspberry Pi irrespective of the port that is used.

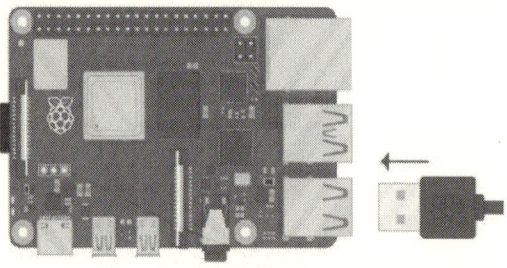

- The keyboard can also be connected in the same way.

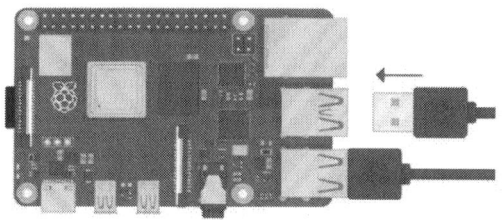

- Ensure that you have your screen plugged into a wall socket, and then switch it on.
- On the HDMI ports available on the Raspberry Pi, you will notice a flat side on the top.
- You can then make use of a cable in connecting the screen to your Raspberry Pi's HDMI port or make use of the adapter if the need arises.

For Raspberry Pi 4

- Connect your screen first via the ports labeled HDMI0 on your Raspberry Pi 4.

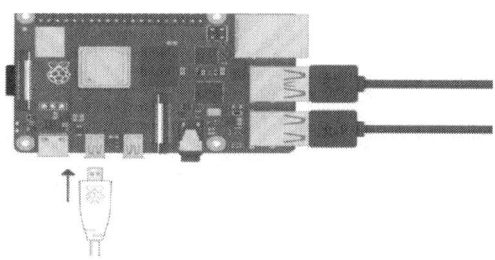

- The second screen should be connected similarly.

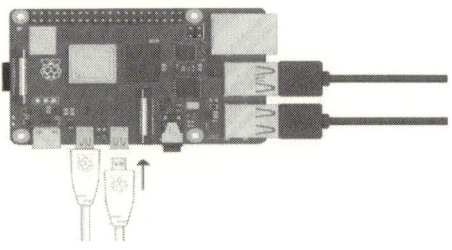

Raspberry Pi 1, 2, 3

- Get your screen connected to the single HDMI port.

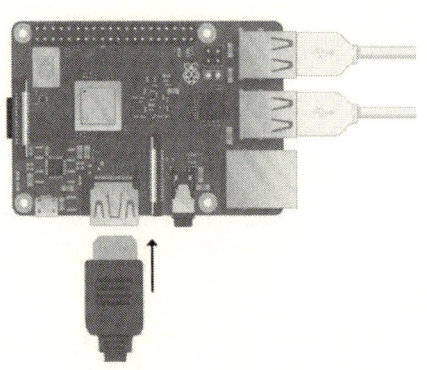

- It should be noted that nothing will show up on your screen simply because the Raspberry Pi is not running yet.
- In a situation where you like to connect your Raspberry to the internet making use of the Ethernet, make use of the Ethernet cable in

connecting the Ethernet port on the Raspberry to an Ethernet socket on the wall or using a router.

- On the other hand, if you are making use of wireless connectivity you won't need to go through the steps above.

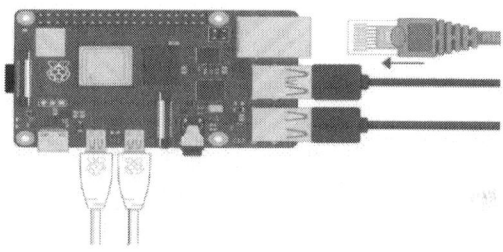

- If there are in-built speakers available on your screen, you will get to play sounds but if not, you can get headphones or speakers connected to the audio port.

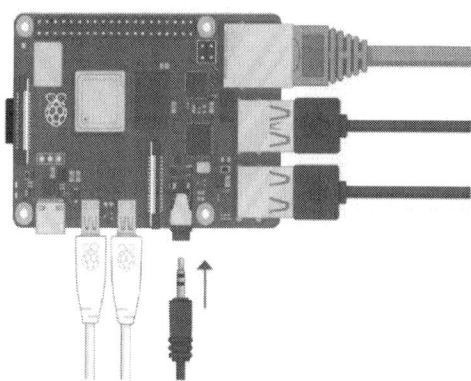

Chapter 4: Starting Up Your Raspberry Pi 4

There is no power switch available on your Raspberry Pi, so anytime it is connected to a power outlet it will be turned on automatically. Once the Raspberry Pi 4 is turned on, a red LED light will come up to indicate that it is connected to power.

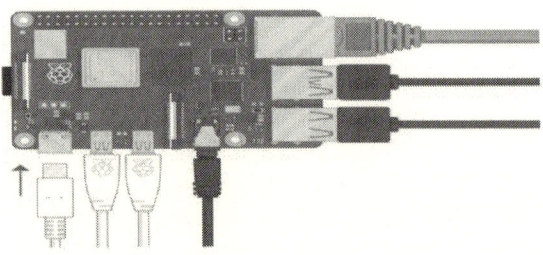

While booting, the raspberries will come up in the top left hand of the screen.

The First-Time Startup Using The NOOBS

i. If you are starting up your Raspberry Pi for the first time with the SD card containing NOOBS, you will be prompted with the NOOBS installer.

ii. The installer will walk you through on getting the Raspbian operating system installed.

iii. Once the installer has been loaded, you will be prompted to select the OS you like to install.

iv. Check the box for Raspbian.

v. Select install.

Finishing the Setup

- The welcome to Raspberry Pi application will come up and lead you through initial setup if you are starting up your Raspberry for the first time.
- Select "Next" to start the setup process.
- Set your Country, Language as well as Timezone.

- Select "Next" again.

- Enter a new password for your Raspberry Pi and select "Next."

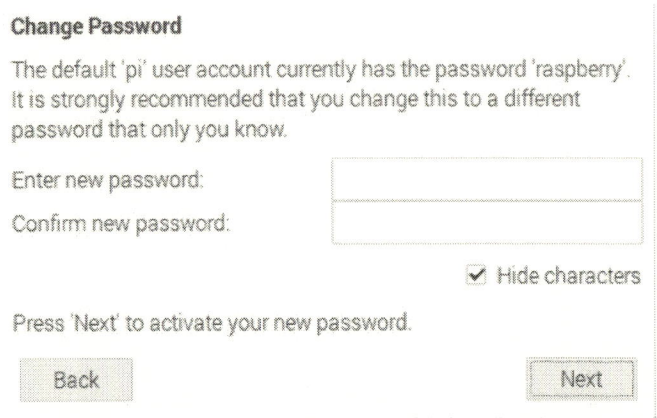

- Get connected to your Wi-Fi network by selecting its name and also inputting your password and click Next. It is to be noted that if your Raspberry model does not have wireless connectivity, this will not come up on your screen.

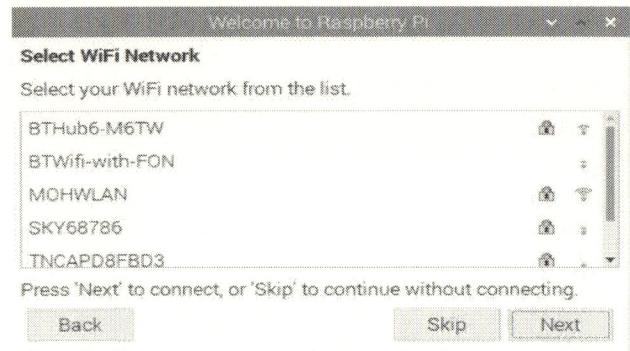

- Select "Next" for the wizard to check for updates to Raspbian and get them installed. It should be noted that this can take some time.

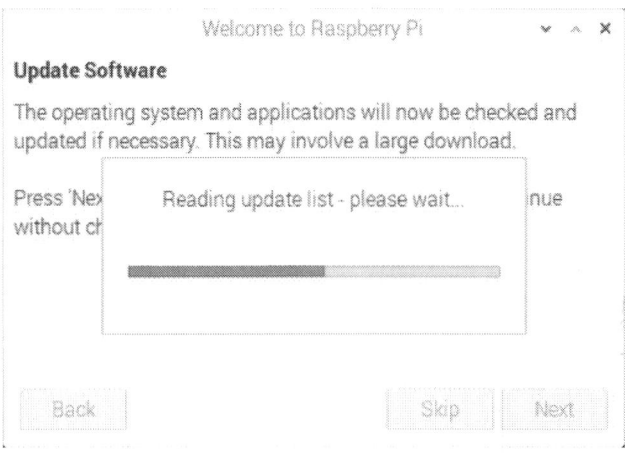

- Select "Done" or Reboot to complete the setup. It is, however, advisable to reboot to help complete the update process.

Chapter 5: Raspberry Pi Desktop

Recall that the Raspberry Pi runs Raspbian which is a version of an operating called the Linux

The desktop will be displayed after the Raspbian starts up.

You will see the Raspberry Pi icon at the top left-hand corner. This is where you can access the menu.

- Click on the icon to help you in accessing lots of applications as well as Programming and office applications.
- Click on Accessories and select the Text Editor to launch a text editor.

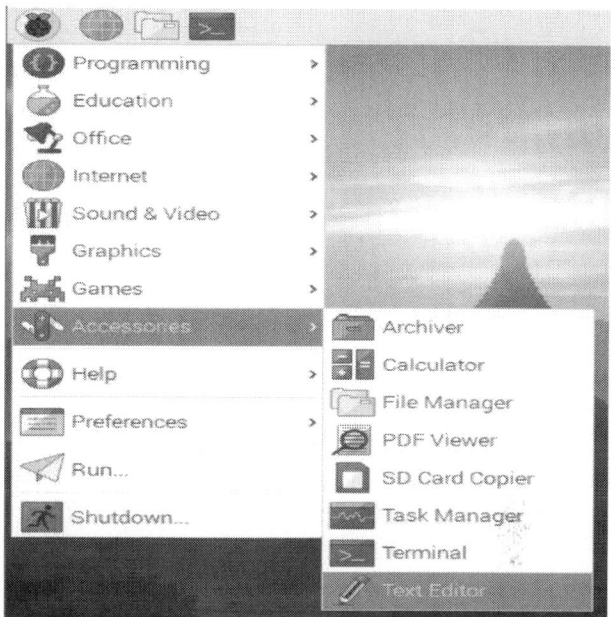

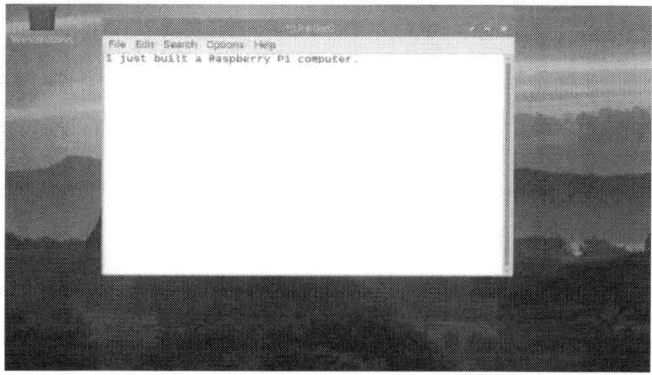

- Click on the x sign located at the top right-hand corner of the window to close the text editor.
- You can also get to explore other available applications on the menu such as the Python games.

Keyboard and Mouse Settings

Select "Preferences" and then the Mouse keyboard settings from the menu to have access to set up your mouse and keyboard.

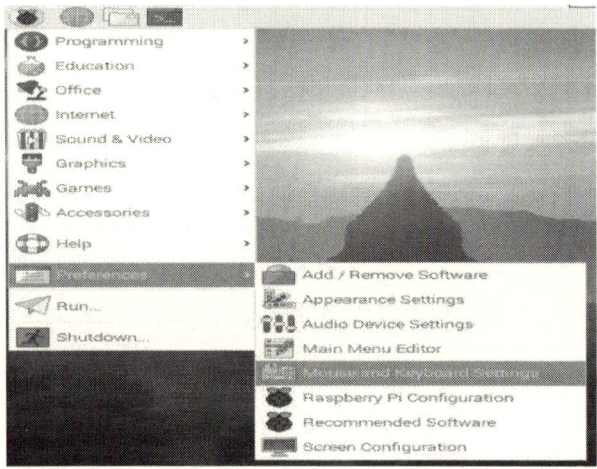

Mouse

The mouse speed can be changed here as well as the double-click time. You can also get to swap the buttons in a situation where you are left-handed.

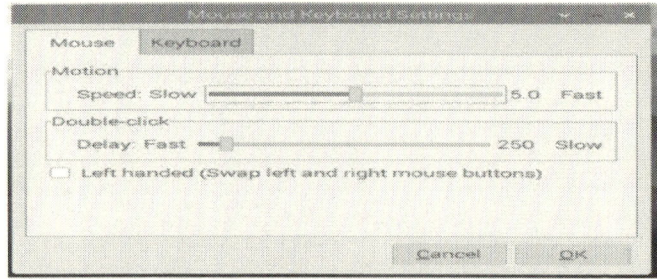

Keyboard

- The Key repeat delay, as well as the interval values can be adjusted here.

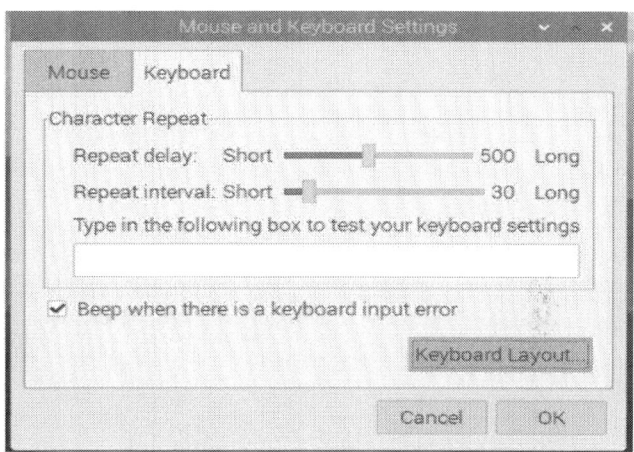

- Select the Keyboard Layout and choose your layout form from the list of countries to help in changing the keyboard layout.

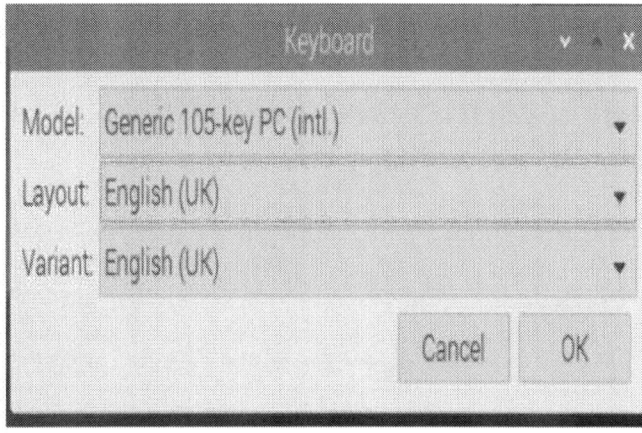

Chapter 6: Connecting To the Internet

To get your Raspberry Pi 4 connected to the internet, you can connect an Ethernet cable into it. On the other hand, if you are using the Pi Zero, there will be a need for a USB-to-Ethernet adaptor too. If you have Pi 4, 3, or Pi Zero W, you can connect to the internet to them using the wireless network.

Connecting To a Wireless Network

- On the top right-hand corner of the screen, click on the wireless network icon and then select your preferred network from the drop-down menu.

- Input in your wireless network password and click "OK"

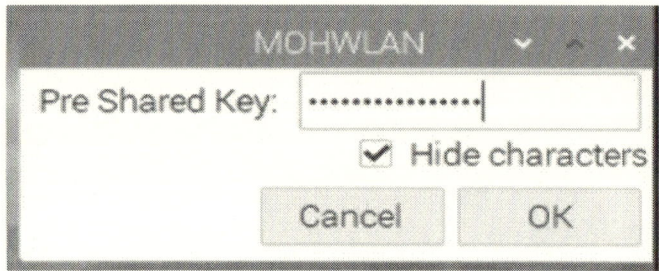

- Once your Pi has been connected to the internet, you will be prompted with a wireless LAN symbol instead of the red crosses.

- To test your connection, click on the web browser icon and browse the web for Raspberry Pi.

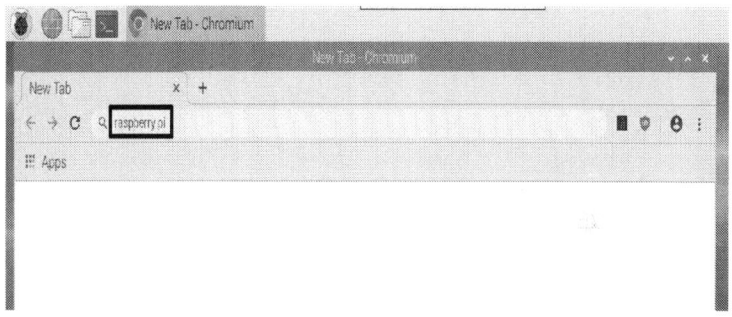

Setting up The Sound

The Raspberry Pi is capable of sending sound to the built-in speakers available on the screen using the HDMI connection. They can also send sounds to the analog headphone jack.

Go to the top right-hand corner and right-click on the speaker icon to choose if your Pi should make use of the HDMI or the analog connection of sound.

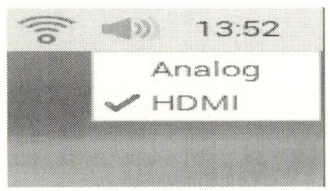

- Select the speaker icon and move the slider up or down to help in adjusting the volume of the speaker.

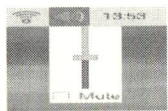

Installing Software

- It is important to note that your Raspberry Pi must be connected to the internet before you can get to install software programs and applications.
- Go to the menu and select "Preferences"
- Select "Recommended Software"

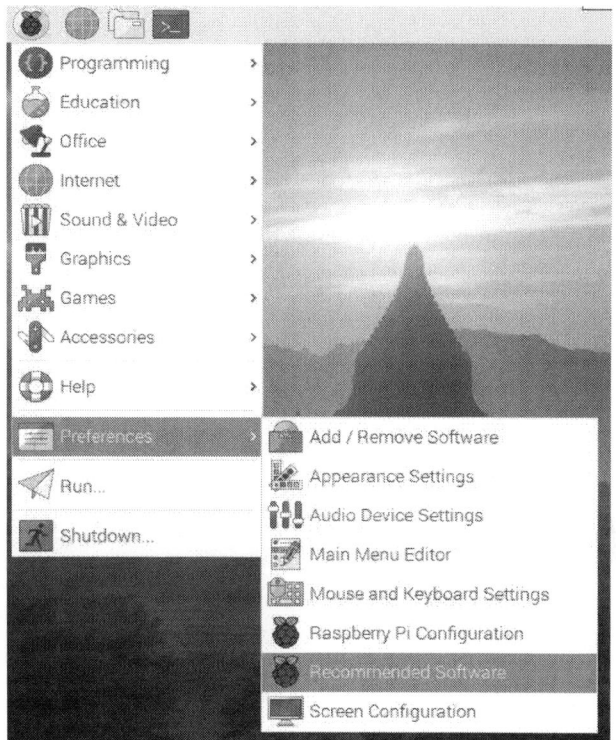

- You will then be prompted with the recommended software from which you can browse and you can also get to filter it by category.

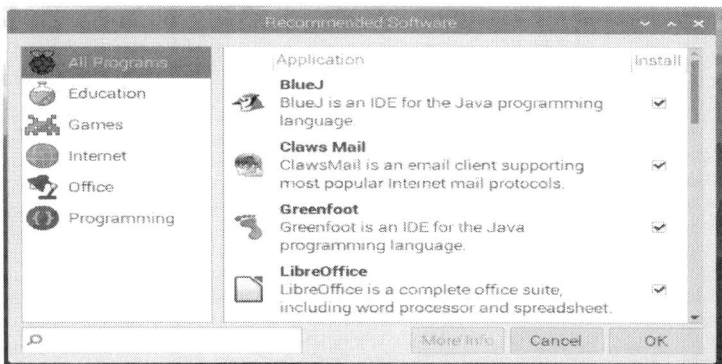

- Click to mark a software checkbox to the right to install it.

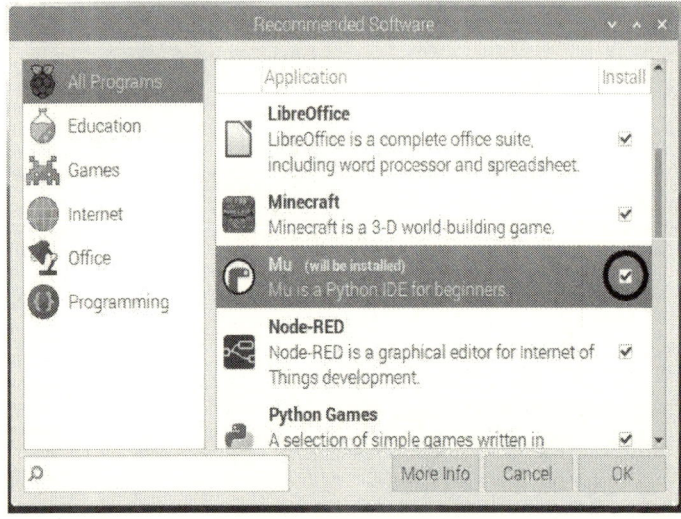

- Click "OK" to have the selected software installed.
- Apart from the software recommended in the Raspberry Pi, there are also other available programs and applications in the library.
- Click on "Preferences"
- Select Add/Remove software option on the menu.

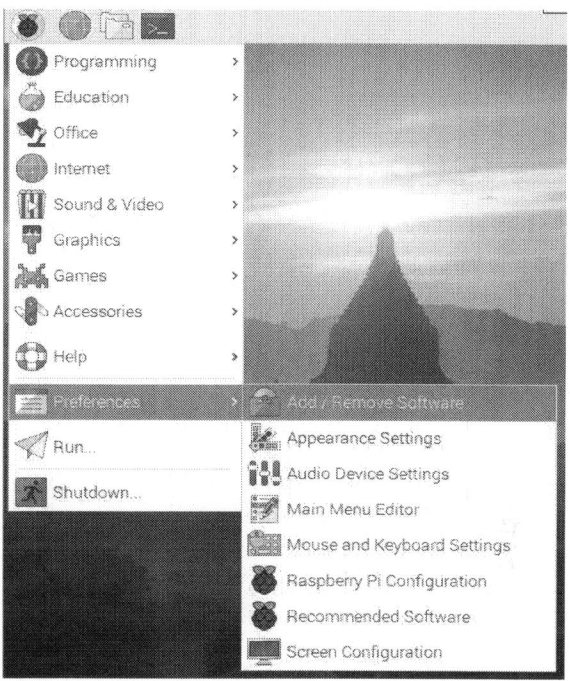

- Select and browse a category from the menu located on the left to search for software.

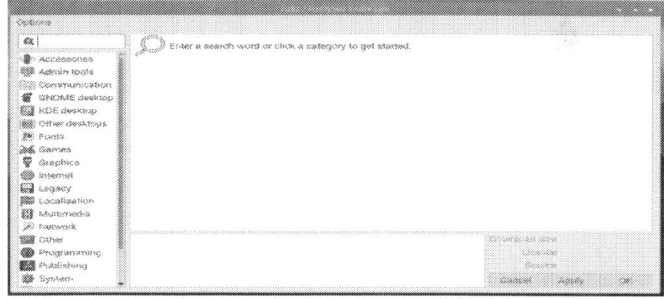

Installing a Drawing Application Called Pinta

i. Type 'pinta' into the search box.

ii. Select Enter.

iii. A list will appear from which you will select "Simple drawing/paint program"

iv. Select "OK" to begin the installation process.

v. Enter a password when prompted.

vi. Once you type in the right password, pinta will get downloaded and installed.

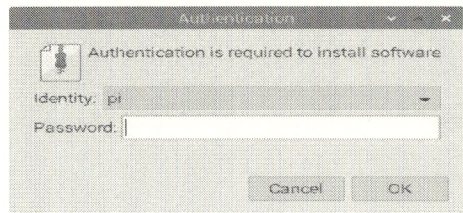

vii. After the installation process is complete, launch Pinta by selecting Graphics and go to the menu to select Pinta.

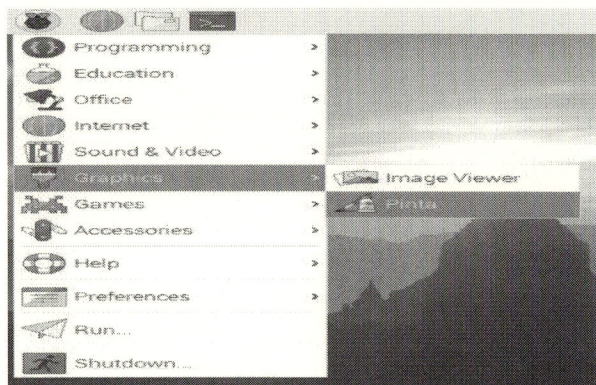

Chapter 7: Updating and Upgrading Raspbian

This section explains how to get software updates deployed to devices running Raspbian. It is important to keep your devices updated due to the following reasons:

- Getting your device updated helps in keeping it secured.
- Once your device gets updated with Raspbian, you will get access to millions of lines of codes that you will need.
- These million lines of codes will, in turn, expose you to well-known vulnerabilities which are known as Common Vulnerabilities and Exposures (CVE).
- These codes are easy to exploit since they are made available and documented in publicly available databases.
- By making sure that your software is up to date as a user of the Raspbian, you will be able to mitigate these exploits. The upstream repositories do track the CVEs closely to mitigate them quickly as well.
- By keeping your software up to date will also help in limiting the chances of hitting bugs which can end up affecting the desired functionality.

Updating your Raspberry Pi

- The Add/Remove software application can be used in updating your Pi.
- Select the Preference section of the menu to gain access to the Add/Remove software application.

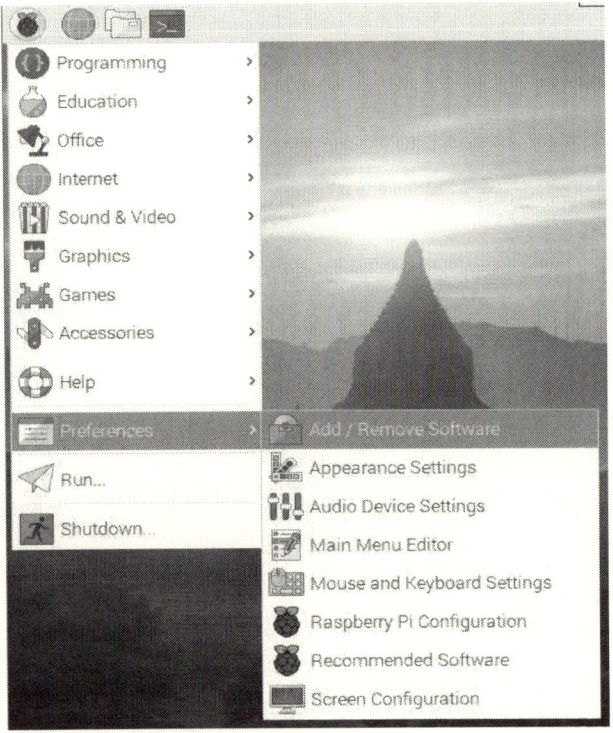

- Make sure you get the software package lists refreshed on your Pi before checking and installing updates.
- Go to the top left-hand corner to click Options

- Select "Refresh Package Lists"

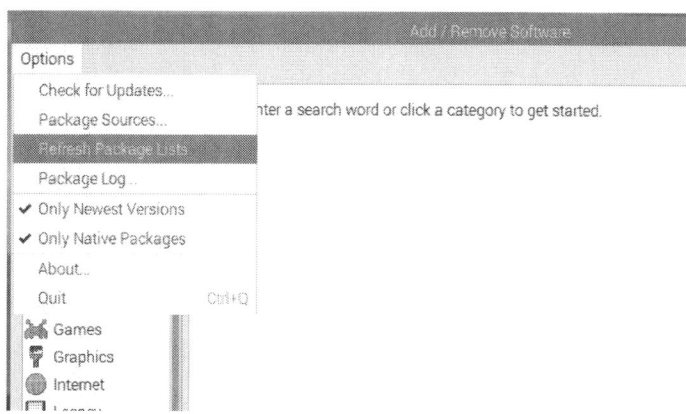

- Your Raspberry Pi will then update all the lists of your packages.

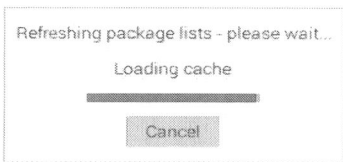

- As soon as the update is complete, click on Options then select the Check for updates option.

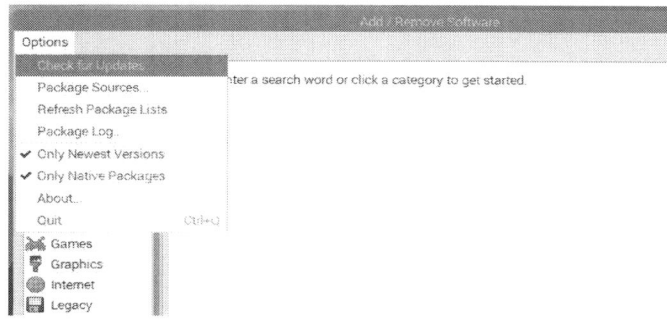

- The Package Updater will get opened automatically and also check if there is another update available. Anything that is found on the list will be displayed.

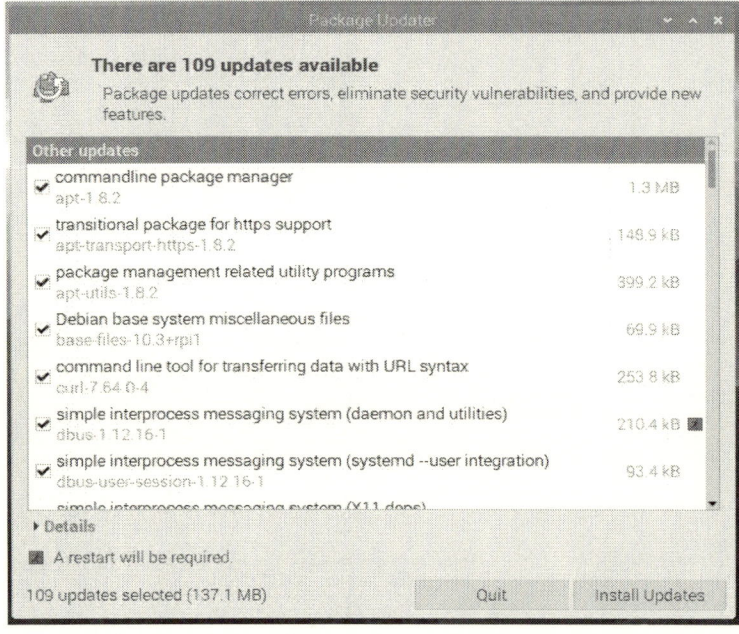

- Select the Install Update option to help install all the available updates.
- Input in your password as soon as you are prompted.

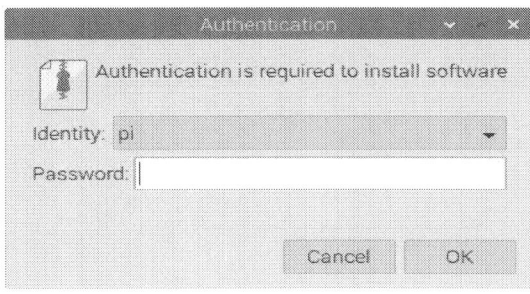

- All updates available will be downloaded and installed. You will get to see your installation by going to the bottom left-hand corner to check the progress bar.

Advanced Packaging Tool (APT)

The Apt tool can be used in a terminal to help update your software in Raspbian.

i. From the application menu or taskbar, open a terminal window.

ii. Enter the command "sudo apt-get update" to get your system's package updated.

iii. Enter the command "sudo apt-get dist-upgrade" to get all your installed packages upgraded to their latest versions.

Doing this regularly will help keep the installations in the Raspbian up to date for a major release such as the Stretch but won't update for a major release to another such as for Stretch to Buster.

It is important to note that occasional changes are made in the foundation's Raspbian image which will require manual intervention such as the newly introduced package. This is because they are not installed with an upgrade.

Also, note that the command mentioned above are only used to upgrade packages that have been installed already.

Updating the Kernel and Firmware

Since the kernel and firmware are both installed as a Debian package, they will automatically get updated when you use the commands above. They get updated frequently after extensive testing.

Running Out Of Space

- The amount of data to be downloaded including the space it will take up in the SD card will be displayed when running the command "sudo apt-get dist-upgrade."
- It is advisable to check if you have enough free disk space using df-h because the apt will not be doing this for you.
- All downloaded packages files (.deb files) are stored in the /var/cache/apt/archives. Nevertheless, this can be removed to free up space by using the command sudo apt-get clean.

Upgrading from Jessie to Stretch

It is possible to upgrade an existing Jessie image but note that this will not work in every circumstance. It is therefore advisable to back up your data first before upgrading a Jessie image to stretch to avoid the loss of data in a situation where there is a failed update.

i. Before upgrading, modify the files /etc/apt/sources.list as well as /etc/apt/sources.list.d/raspi.list.

ii. Change everywhere you have Jessie to stretch and it is to be noted that sudo will be required to edit in both files.

iii. Launch the terminal window and run the command; sudo apt-get update and sudo apt-get –y dist-upgrade.

iv. For any prompt that comes up, reply with "yes."

v. At some point, the installation might pause while page information is shown on the screen, when this happens; hold the space key to scroll through and press "q" to continue.

vi. If the PulseAudio is only used for Bluetooth and nothing else, remove it from the image by entering the command sudo apt-get –y purge "pulseaudio"

If you are changing to a new Pi model such as the Pi 3B+, the kernel and the firmware may need to be updated as well by following the instructions above.

Third-Party Solutions

For any device running the Raspbian, Apt is a convenient way for updating the software, but this method is limited when you have a larger pool of devices to update especially when there is no physical access to your devices and are distributed geographically.

In a situation where you don't have physical access to your device and you need to deploy an unattended Over-The-Air (OTA), the following requirements should be put into consideration:

i. Updating must not break the devices under any circumstances, for instance, when the update is being interrupted due to network or power loss, the system should fall back into a working state.

ii. The updating must be atomic. And either the update succeeded or failed, nothing in between can result in a device still functioning but it will exhibit undefined behavior.

iii. The updating process must be able to have images or packages that are cryptographically signed installed thereby preventing third parties from gaining access to install software on your device.

iv. The updating process must be able to have updates installed using a secure communication channel.

Generally, apt is lacking in terms of robustness features that are atomicity and fall-back.

This is the reason third-party solutions have been creating solutions to problems that need attention for deploying unattended updates OTA.

Mender

This can be referred to as an end-to-end, open-source update manager. The atomic dual system update helps in providing a robust update process with the availability of a working system partition. The Mender then updates the one that is not running

Chapter 8: How to Access Your Files

The MicroSD card is responsible for storing all your Raspberry Pi files including the ones that were created by you. Select "Accessories" and Go to the menu and select the File Manager or go to the menu bar to select the File Manager.

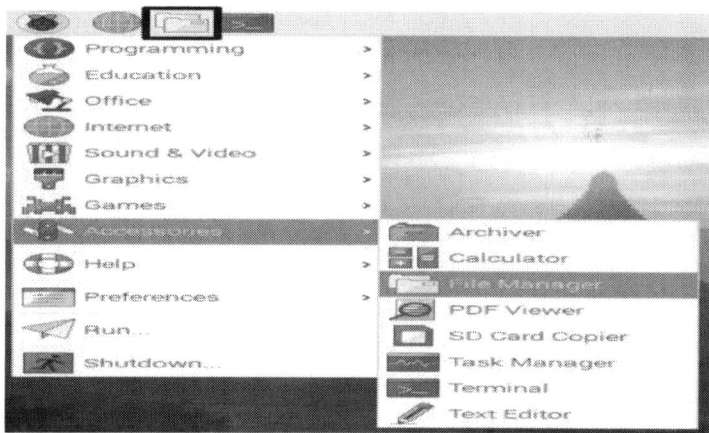

As soon as the File manager comes up, it will display the Pi directory where your files can be stored as well as creating a new subfolder.

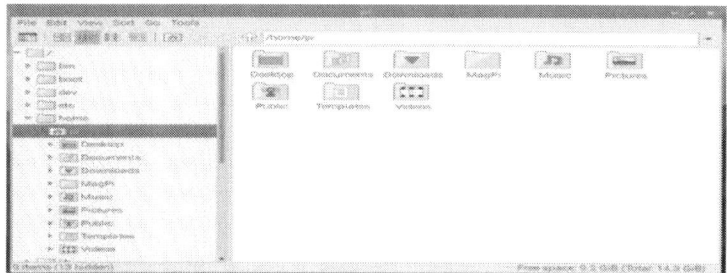

The following are the main subdirectories:

Desktop: This is the folder you will see when you load the Raspbian. In a situation where you have a file saved here, it will be displayed on the Raspbian desktop for easy access and loading.

Documents: This is the home to most of the files that you will create such as recipes, short stories, etc.

Download: Any file that is downloaded from the internet via your Chromium browser will be automatically saved in the Downloads.

MagPi: This is referred to as the official Raspberry Pi' magazine and it contains an electronic copy of the MagPi.

Music: Music that is created and kept on the Raspberry Pi is saved here/

Pictures: In technical terms, pictures are referred to as image files and they are saved here.

Public: However, it is to be noted that most of your files are private but any file that has been designated as public will be made available to other Raspberry Pi users even if there are username and password attached.

Videos: This is the first location for most video-playing programs and it is the folder where videos are kept.

Generally, the file manager window can be split into two panes: which are the left and the right pane.

i. The left pane will display the directories available on your Raspberry Pi

ii. The right pane will display the files and subdirectories of the directory which are selected in the left pane.

In case a removable storage device is plugged into the USB port of the Raspberry Pi, you will be prompted by a pop-up window asking if you would like to have it open in the File manager. Once this pop up comes up, select OK for you to view the files and directories.

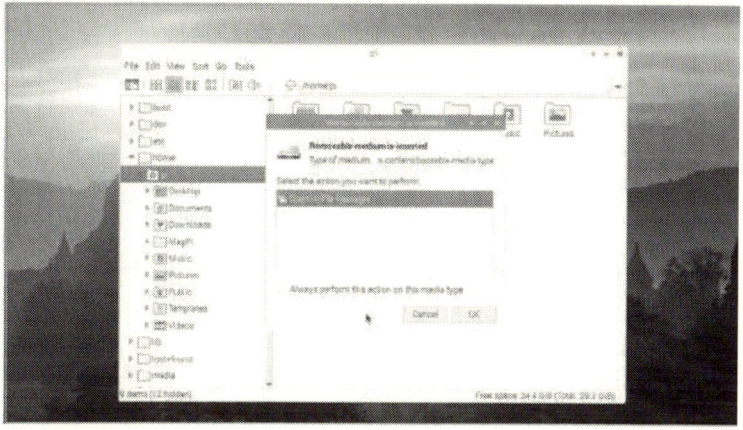

To open the directory and view the files available in it, double-click on the Documents icon.

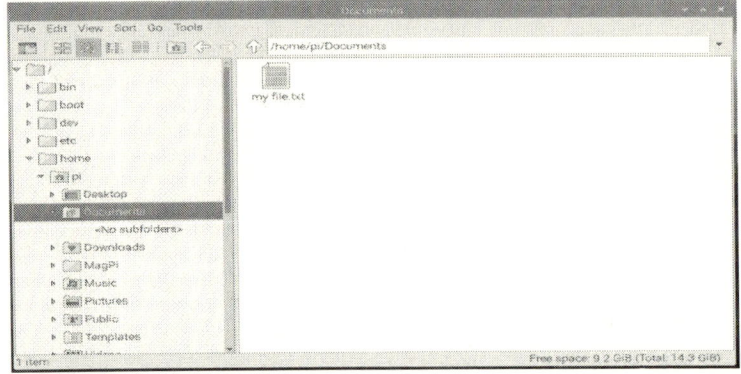

To get a file opened, double click on the file's name. You can alternatively right-click the file to open the file menu for more options.

The Raspberry Pi supports the use of USB drives and sticks which make backups and copying of files to another computer easy.

Once you get a USB stick inserted into your Raspberry Pi, you will be prompted on the screen by a window asking what action you would love to perform. Open the File Manager by clicking OK.

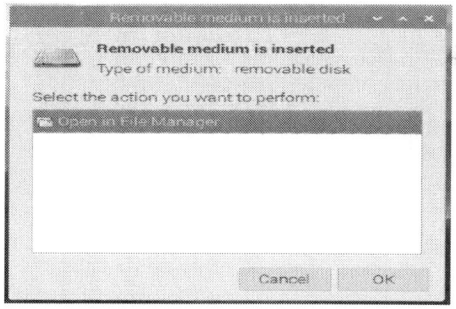

The File Manager will be automatically opened showing you the available files on your USB stick.

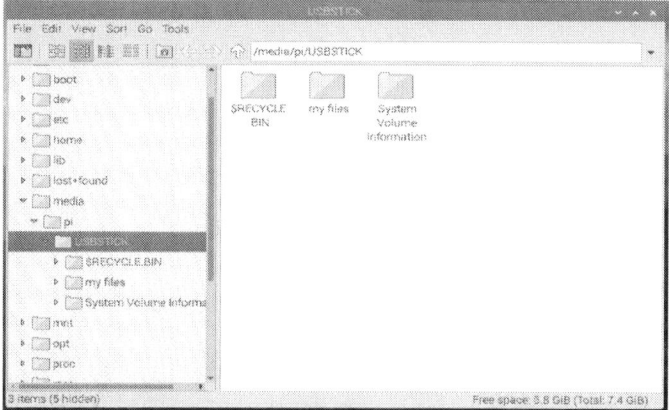

Keyboard Shortcuts

Keyboard shortcut such as the CTRL+C means having the first key which is CTRL on the keyboard held down and then pressing C which is the second key and then, finally releasing both of the keys.

Once you are done with the File Manager, select the close button at the top left to close the window. In a case where you have multiples window opened, close them all.

If a removable storage device is connected to your Raspberry Pi, you can get it ejected by selecting the eject button located at the screen's top right, select it from the list and click on it before getting it unplugged.

Ejecting Devices

Before unplugging an external storage device, always remember to make use of the eject button to avoid your files from getting corrupted and unusable.

Chapter 9: Using the Terminal

The terminal application is very useful in different ways. It helps you in the navigation of file directories as well as the control of your Pi with the use of commands instead of having to click on the menu options.

- To get the terminal window opened, select the Terminal icon located at the top of the screen. Alternatively, you can select the Accessories then go to the menu to select Terminal.

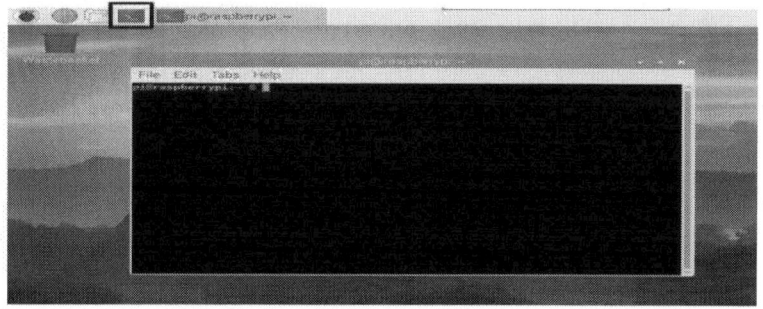

- Commands can be inputted into the terminal window. Press enter on your keyboard to run the command entered.
- Type "ls" in the terminal window and select Enter on the keyboard.
- The command 'ls' will have all the files and subdirectory in the current file directory listed. The

File directory that is accessed by the terminal when it is opened is called Pi and it opens up by default.

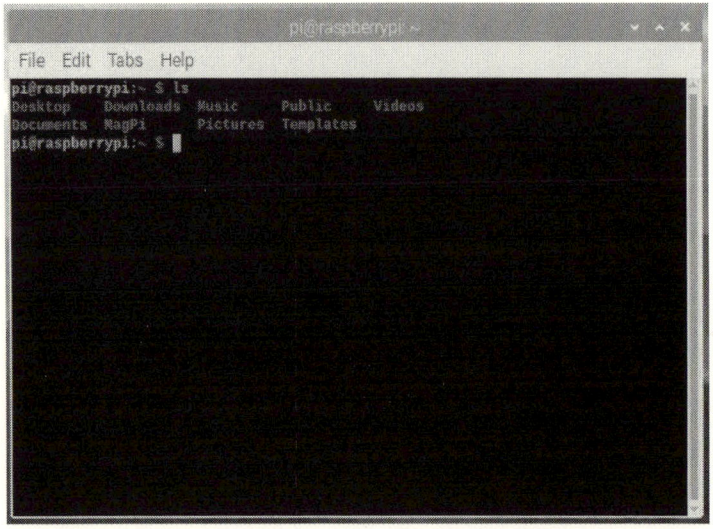

- Type in the command "cd Desktop" to help in changing directory to the Desktop. And remember to press enter on the keyboard to run your command.
- The command 'Is' can be used in listing the files that are available in the Desktop directory.

```
ls
```

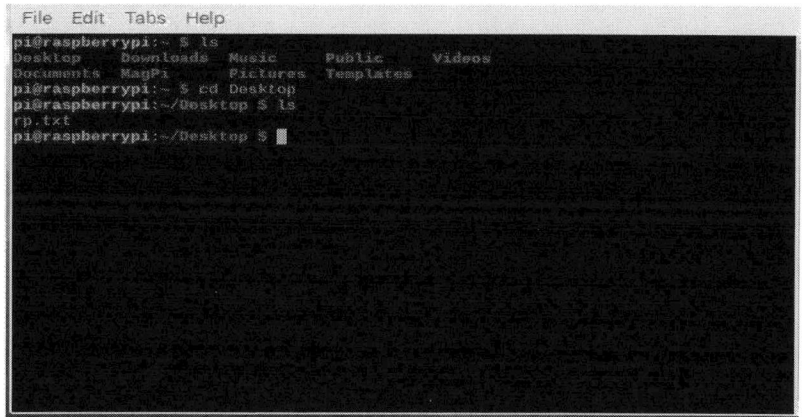

- The terminal is a very powerful tool that enables you to interact with your Raspberry Pi.
- For example, by typing the command pinout, a labeled diagram of the GPIO pins will be displayed including some additional information about your Pi.

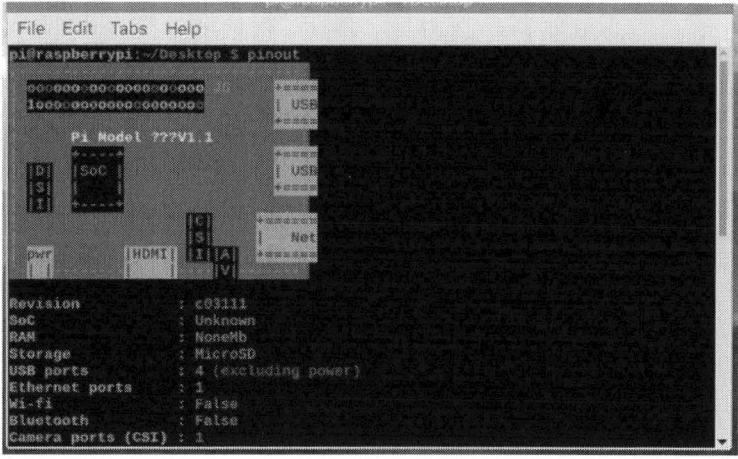

- Click on the x sign or use the command exit to close the terminal window.

Chapter 10: Configuring your Pi

The Configuration application of the Raspberry Pi which is found in the Preferences option of the menu can be used in controlling most of the settings of your Raspberry Pi.

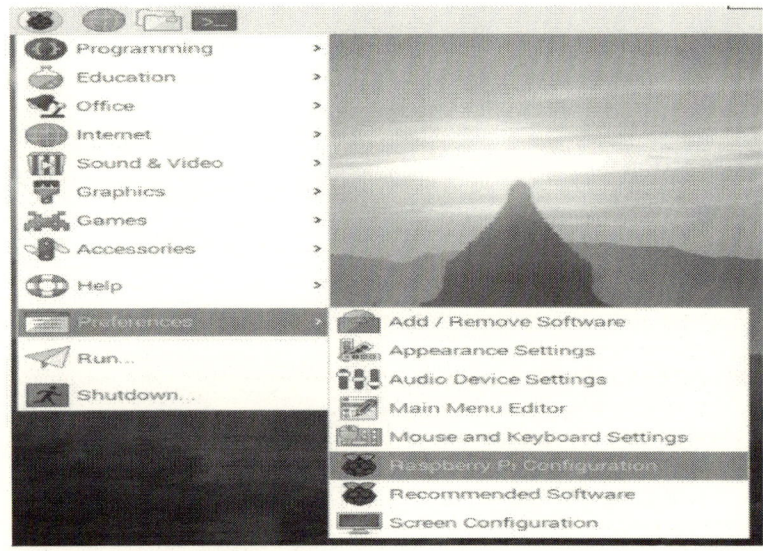

System Tab: This tab enables you to change the basic system settings of your Pi.

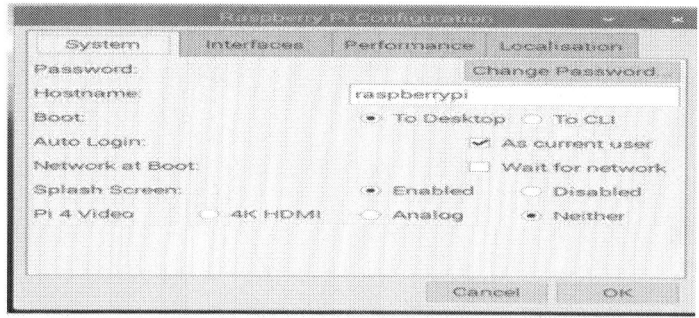

Password: It is advisable to make sure you change the password from raspberry which is the factory default password. All you need to do is set the password of the pi user.

Boot: Select this to display the Desktop or the Command Line Interface when starting up your Raspberry Pi.

Auto Login: With this option enabled, you will be automatically logged in by the Raspberry Pi whenever it starts up.

Network at Boot: Once this option is selected, your Raspberry Pi will wait before starting up until there is a network connection available.

Splash screen: This option enables you to choose whether or not to show the splash or startup screen when the Raspberry Pi boots up.

Interfaces

Devices and components can get linked up to the Raspberry Pi by making use of different connection types. These different connections can be turned on or off using the Interfaces tab thereby enabling your Pi to recognize if it has been linked to through some type of connection.

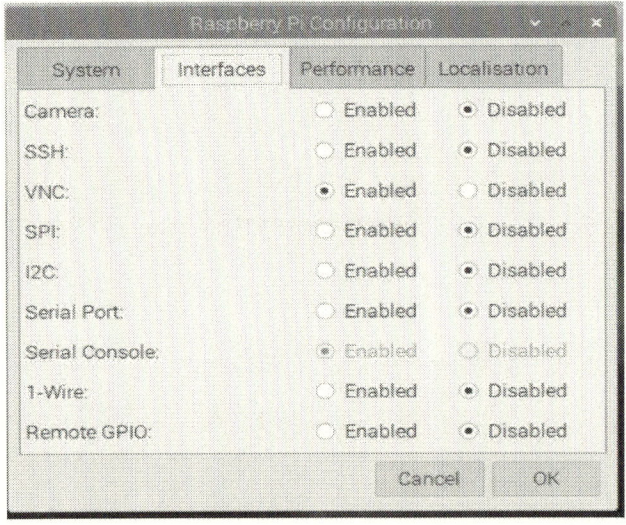

Camera: This enables the Raspberry Pi Camera Module.

SSH: This allows remote access to your Raspberry Pi with the use of SSH from another computer.

VNC: This makes use of the VNC in allowing remote access to your Raspberry Pi Desktop from a different computer.

SPI: This activates the SPI GPIO pins.

12C: This is used in enabling the 12C GPIO pins.

Serial: This enables the Serial (Rx, Tx) GPIO pins.

1-Wire: This helps in enabling the 1-wire GPIO pin.

Remote GPIO: This allows you to access the GPIO pins of your Raspberry Pi from a different computer.

Performance

The performance settings of your Raspberry Pi can be changed using this tab if you have a particular project to work on. Nevertheless, it is important to note that changing the performance of your Raspberry Pi's setting can cause it to behave irregularly or not working.

Overclock: This helps in changing the speed and voltage of your CPU to increase performance.

GPU Memory: This changes the allocation of memory that is given to the GPU.

Localization

With this tab, you can easily change the settings of your Raspberry Pi into a specific country or location.

Locale: This is used to set your Raspberry Pi's language, the country as well as the character set.

Time zone: With this, you can set the time zone of your Pi.

Keyboard: This is used in changing the layout of your keyboard.

Wi-Fi Country: This is used in setting the country code of your Wi-Fi.

Chapter 11: The Chromium Web Browser

The Chromium browser is a web browser that allows you to visit websites, play video games and get to interact with people far and wide on forums as well as chat sites. You can start to use your Chromium by simply maximizing its window to take up the screen.

i. Load the Chromium browser to start up with practicing the use of your Raspberry Pi.

ii. Go to the top left and click on the raspberry icon to display the menu.

iii. Select the internet category using your mouse pointer.

iv. Select the Chromium web browser to get it loaded.

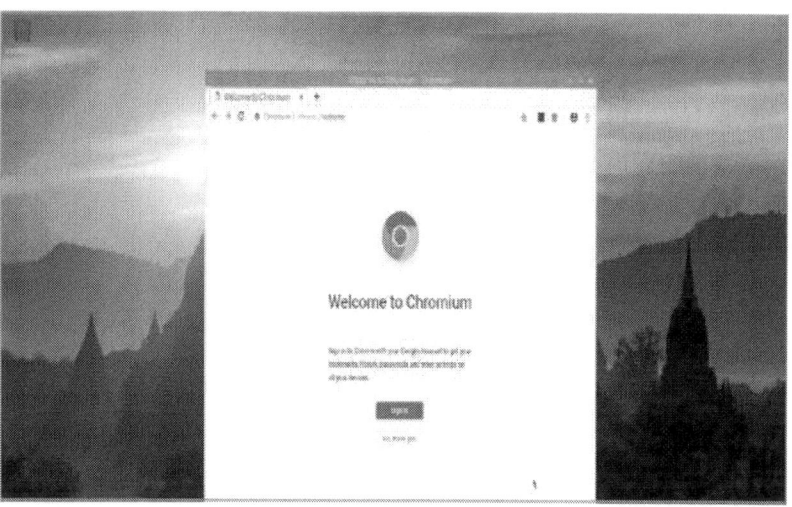

- Go to the top right of the chromium window title bar, where you will find three icons. Select the middle one denoted by an up-arrow icon. This will help in maximizing the window such that it will fill up the screen.
- Next to the maximize button to the left, is the minimize button that helps in hiding a window until you select it on the taskbar located at the top screen to have it opened again.
- The icon to the right of the maximize button is the close button, as the name implies, it will close the window.

CLOSE AND SAVE

While most programs will warn you to save before closing your work whenever you select the close button, some will not warn you. So, it is advisable to make sure you save your works before closing it.

To start exploring your chromium-browser:

i. Go to the address bar which is located at the top of the Chromium window which is the big white bar having a magnifying glass on the left-hand side.

ii. Type in a website address and tap the ENTER key on your keyboard. This will load the website.

iii. Several tabs might come up at the top of the window if you are loading chromium for the first time.

iv. To go to a different tab, select the tab in question.

v. Click on the cross icon which is located at the right-hand edge of the tab you like to close to get it closed.

vi. Click on the tab button located at the right of the last tab on the list to open a new tab alternatively, you can have the CTRL key on the keyboard held down and press the "T" key before releasing your finger on the CTRL.

vii. As soon as you are done exploring your Chromium web browser, click on the close button which is located at the top right of the window.

Chapter 12: Programming With Scratch

The Raspberry Pi is a whole new experience. It's more than just using software; you get to do things you cannot do with software created by others. The best part is that you do not need experience in coding (creating your programs) to explore, create and experiment with the Raspberry Pi.

All you need to optimize this platform is a certain visual programming language known as Scratch. Developed by the Massachusetts Institute of Technology (MIT), Scratch makes building programs fun since it allows you to build using pre-written chunks of code known as blocks.

Scratch is the perfect programming language because it combines power with ease of use.

How?

With Scratch, coders have a user-friendly experience that is as powerful as it is functional. So whether you are a newbie or veteran coder, you will have access to an environment that allows you to create just about anything you want from basic computer games and animations to advanced level interactive robotics projects.

The Scratch 2 interface

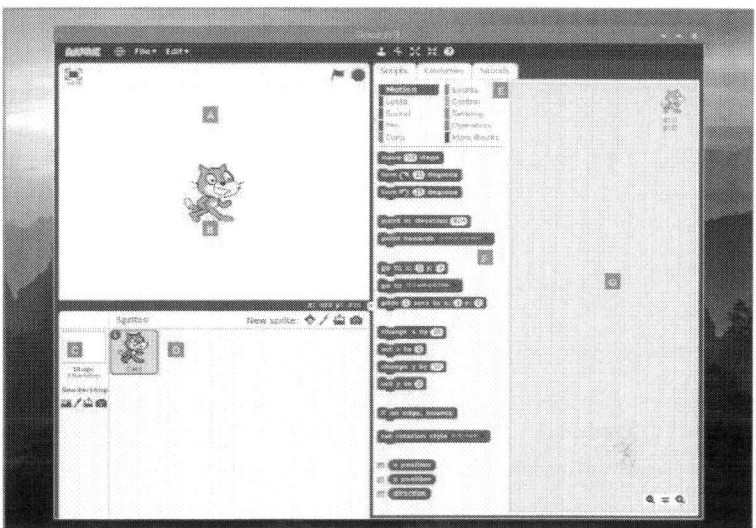

A. Stage Area – Your sprites are controlled by your program but they move around the way actors in a play and move around the stage area.

B. Sprite – This is another name for the characters or objects that are controlled by your Scratch program. They sit on the stage. An example is the meowing cat.

C. Stage Controls – Like with plays, your stage can be modified using your pictures as backgrounds. You can achieve this by using the stage controls.

D. Sprites List –This is a list of all the sprites you created or loaded into the Scratch program. They can be found in a section of the window.

E. Blocks Palette –The block palette features all the blocks available for your program. They are in color-coded categories.

F. Blocks –Blocks are pre-written chunks of program code. Just as in real life, they enable you build your program the way you want, starting from the ground up.

G. Scripts Area – This is the area where you build your program using blocks that you drag and drop from the blocks palette.

Scratch 3

You can now install and use Scratch 3 Desktop for Raspbian on your Raspberry Pi 4

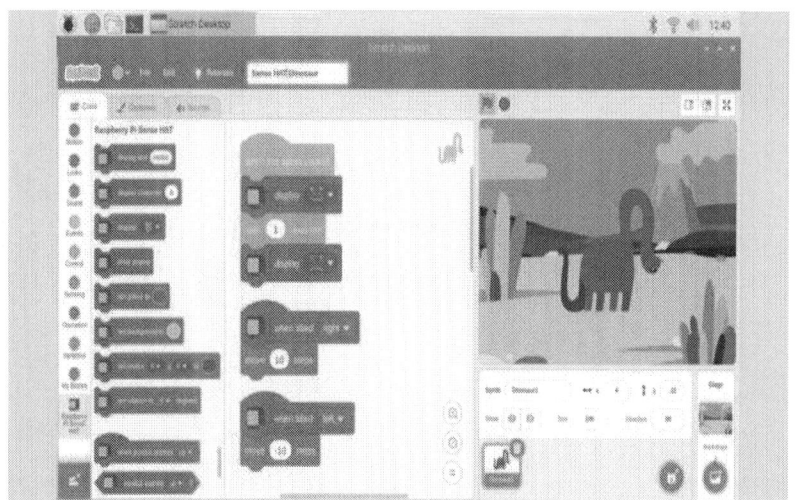

Scratch 3 was released in January this year, 2019. And since then the Scratch team have put lots of work into creating an offline version for Raspberry Pi. The new version of Scratch has a significantly improved interface and better functionality compared to previous versions.

These improvements come at the cost of needing more processing power to run. Luckily, Raspberry Pi 4 has delivered just that, and with the software improvements in the newest version of Raspbian, Buster, we can now deliver a reliable Scratch 3 experience on our computer.

Which Raspberry Pi can I use?

Scratch 3 needs at least 1GB of RAM to run, and we recommend a Raspberry Pi 4 with at least 2GB RAM. While you can run Scratch 3 on a Raspberry Pi 2, 3, 3B+, or a Raspberry 4 with 1GB RAM, performance on these models is reduced, and depending on what other software you run at the same time, Scratch 3 may fail to start due to lack of memory.

The Scratch team is working to reduce the memory requirements of Scratch 3, so we will hopefully see improvements to this soon.

How to install Scratch 3

You can only install Scratch 3 on Raspbian Buster. First, update Raspbian!

If you've yet to upgrade to Raspbian Buster, we recommend installing a fresh version of Buster onto your SD card instead of upgrading from your current version of Raspbian. If you're already using Raspbian Buster, but you're not sure you're running the latest version, update Buster.

Once you're running the latest version of Buster, you can install Scratch 3 either using the Recommended Software application or apt on the terminal.

How to Install Scratch 3 Using the Recommended Software App

Open up the menu, click on Preferences > Recommended Software, and then select Scratch 3 and click on OK.

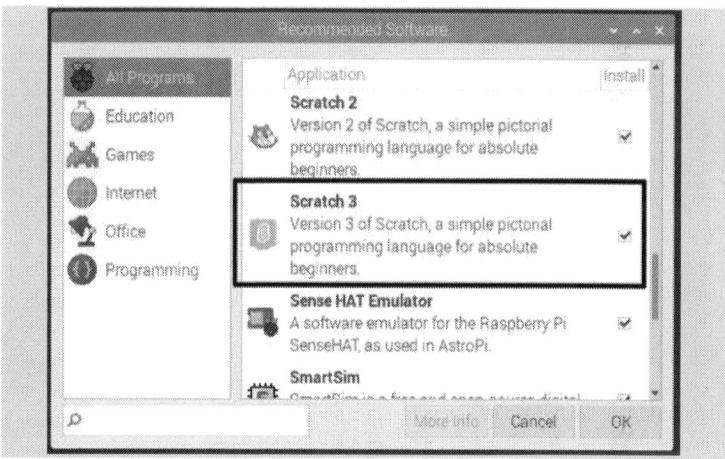

How to Install Scratch 3 Using the Terminal

Open a terminal window, and type in and run the following commands:

```
sudo apt-get update
sudo apt-get install scratch3
```

What can I do with Scratch 3 and Raspberry Pi?

Scratch 3 Desktop for Raspbian comes with new extensions to allow you to control the GPIO pins and Sense HAT with Scratch code!

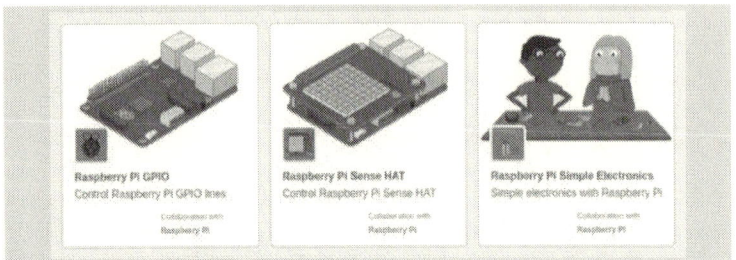

GPIO extension

GPIO extension is a replacement for the existing extension in Scratch 2. Its layout and functionality is very similar, so you can use it as a drop-in replacement.

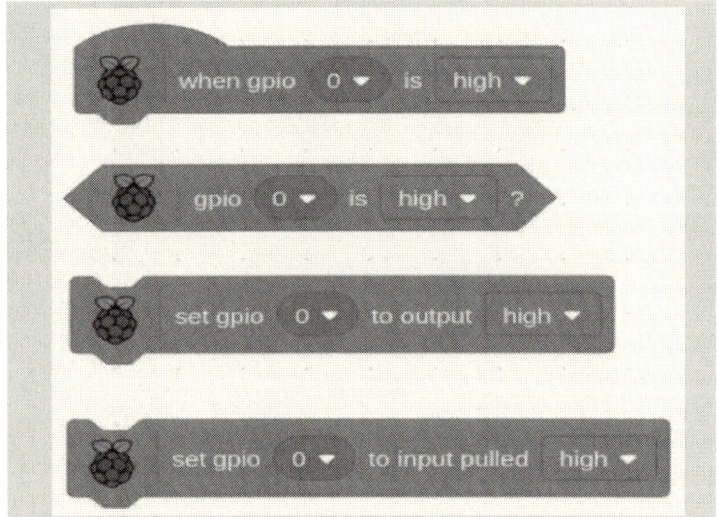

The GPIO extension gives you the flexibility to connect and control a whole host of electronic devices.

Simple Electronics Extension

If you are looking to add something simple, like a LED or button controller for a game, you should find the new Simple Electronics extension easier to use than the GPIO extension. The Simple Electronics extension is the first version of a beginner-friendly extension for interacting with Raspberry Pi's GPIO pins.

Taking lessons from the implementation of gpiozero for Python, this new extension provides a simpler way of using electronic components: currently buttons and LEDs.

In this example, a LED connected to GPIO pin 17 is controlled by a button connected between pin 2 and GND.

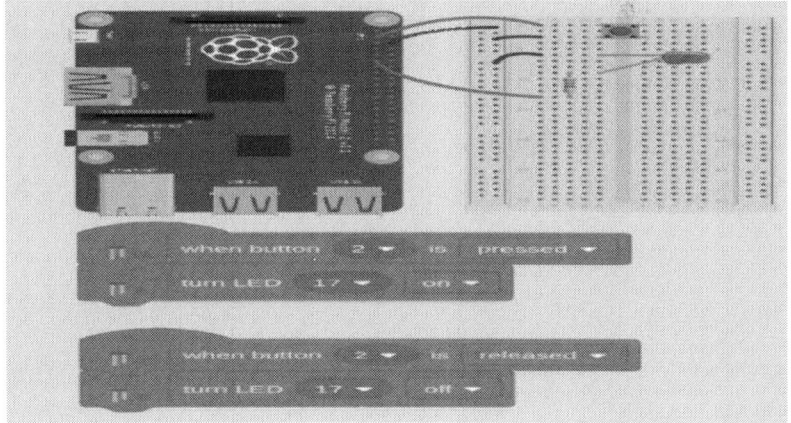

Sense HAT Extension

The company has improved the Sense HAT extension to take advantage of new features in Scratch 3, and the updated version of the extension also introduces a number of new blocks to allow you to:

- Sense tilting, shaking, and orientation
- Use the joystick
- Measure temperature, pressure, and humidity
- Display text, characters, and patterns on the LED matrix

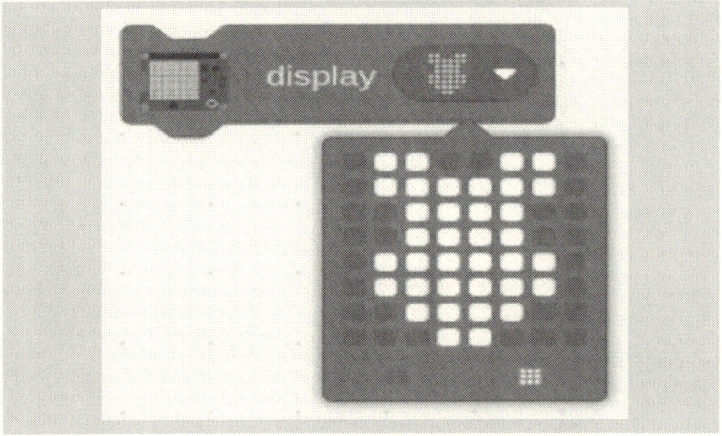

micro:bit and LEGO extensions

The micro:bit and LEGO extensions will become available later on Scratch 3 Desktop. This is because Scratch Link, the software which allows Scratch to talk to Bluetooth devices, is not yet available for Linux-type operating systems like Raspbian.

A version of Scratch Link for Raspbian is part of the plans but, as yet, there is no release date.

Your first Scratch program: Hello, World!

Like with other programs on the Pi, all you have to do to load your Scratch 2 or 3 is to:

1. Click on the raspberry icon to load the Raspbian menu

2. Move the cursor to the Programming section

3. Click on Scratch 2 or 3. Give it a few seconds and voila, the Scratch user interface will load.

Scratch is different from most programming languages because there is no need to give the computer written instructions. Simply:

1. Start by clicking on the Look category in the blocks palette, found in the center of the Scratch window. This brings up the blocks under that category which is cast in purple.

2. Find the say Hello! Block

3. Click and hold the left mouse button on it,

4. Drag it over to the scripts area at the right-hand side of the Scratch window after which you release the mouse button

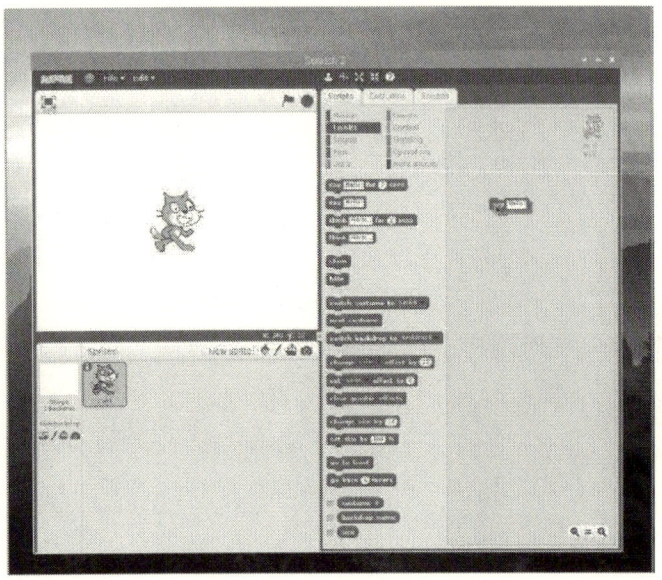

Drag and drop the block into the scripts area

If you take a close look at the block you've just dropped, you will notice that it is similar to a jigsaw puzzle with a hole at the top with a matching part sticking out at the bottom. This suggests that another block can be added above or below. Interestingly, that part that can be added to the top is called a trigger in this program.

In other to continue:

1. Click on the Events category of the blocks palette, which is light brown

2. Click and drag the when **clicked** block – known as a hat block – onto the scripts area.

3. Position it so that the bit sticking out of the bottom connects into the hole at the top of your **say Hello!** block until you see a white outline.

Precision is not the goal here. Just go close enough and the block will snap into place. In the event that it does not drop;

4. Click and hold on it again to adjust its position until it does.

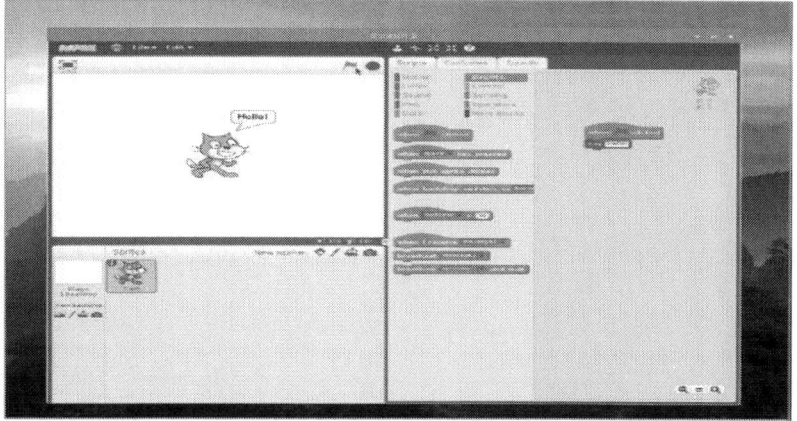

At this point you can "test-run" the program. To do this,

1. Click on the green flag icon at the top of the stage area. If all has gone well, the cat sprite on the stage will greet you with a cheery 'Hello!'

Click on the green flag above the stage and the cat will say 'Hello'

But that's not all!

You should name your program after which you save it. To do this,

1. Click on the File menu, then Save Project.

2. Next, you type in a name

3. Then you click the Save button

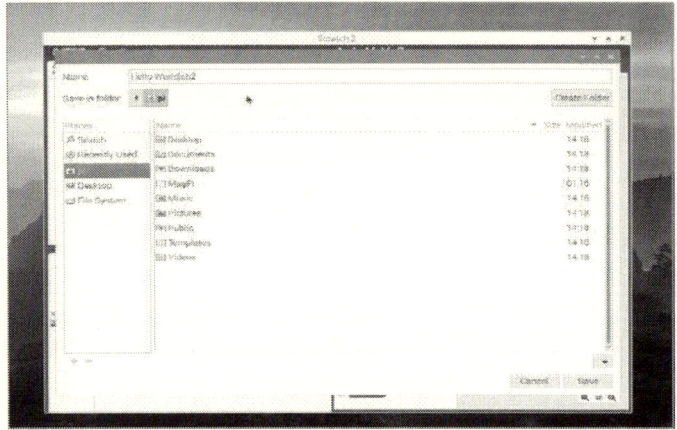

Save your program with a memorable name

WHAT CAN IT SAY?

It is possible to change some blocks Scratch blocks. Just:

1. Click on the word 'Hello!'

2. Type something different

3. Click the green flag once again.

Next Steps: Sequencing

Given that programs are essentially recipes for computers, it is in your best interest to master sequencing since each instruction follows a linear sequence of instructions.

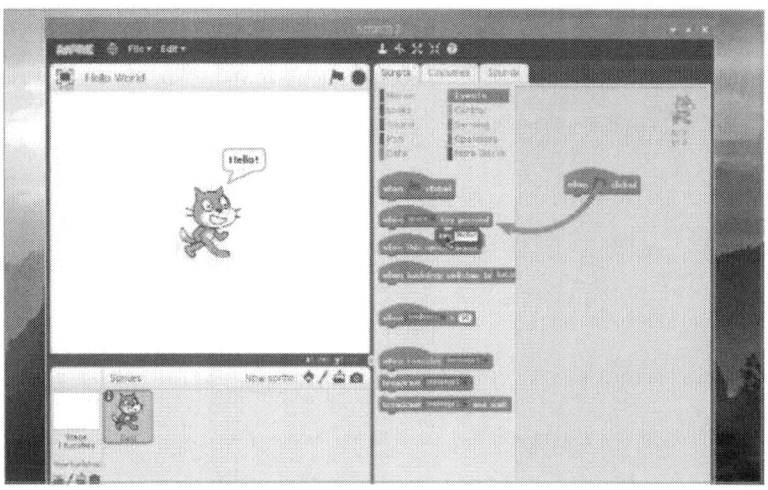

Here's how you go about it,

1. Start by clicking and dragging the say Hello! block from the scripts area back to the blocks palette. This delete the block, removing it from your program and leaving just the trigger block, when clicked.

To delete a block, simply drag it out of the scripts area

2. Click on the Motion category in the blocks palette,

3. Then click and drag the move 10 steps block so it locks into place under the trigger block on the scripts area. This triggers your sprite to move a few steps in its current direction.

In order to create a sequence you should add more instructions to your program.

1. Click on the Sound palette, colour-coded pink

2. Then you click and drag the play sound meow until done block so it locks underneath the move 10 steps block.

3. Go back to the Motion category and drag another move 10 steps block underneath your Sound block.

4. Then click on the '10' to select it and type '-10' to create a `move -10 steps` block.

5. Next you click on the green flag above the stage to run the program. There should be a meowing cat that's moving to the right hear.

6. Click the flag once again. That should make the cat repeat its actions.

So far so good you are now the creator of a sequence of instructions. So while Scratch is quickly running the instructions one at a time from top to bottom, try to delete the `play sound meow until done` block.

1. Click and drag the bottom `move -10 steps` block to detach it.

2. Then drag the `play sound meow until done` block to the blocks palette

3. Then replace it with the simpler `play sound meow` block, after which you

4. Drag your `move -10 steps` block back onto the bottom of your program.

When you click the green flag to run your program again, it might appear as if the sprite isn't moving. The fact is that it is moving so fast that it appears to be standing still.

How, you might ask?

The thing is the Raspberry Pi operates at such a speed that the instructions move much faster than the sprite so the `play sound meow` block doesn't wait for the sound to finish playing before the next step.

Besides using the `play sound meow until done` block, you can correct this by,

1. Clicking on the Control category of the blocks palette, colour-coded gold.

2. Then click and drag a `wait 1 secs` block between the `play sound meow` block and the bottom `move -10 steps` block.

3. The next step is to click the green flag to run your program one last time. At this point a delay should occur.

A "delay" is simply the sprite's movement from right to left amid one-second delays.

This delay helps you to control the length of time the sequence of instructions takes to run.

CHALLENGE: ADD MORE STEPS

You should try to add more steps to your sequence and change the values in the existing steps.

Looping the Loop

The sequence you created has a one track mind. Once you click the green flag, sprite moves and meows, then the program stops. Click the green flag again and the process repeats itself.

Scratch comes with a type of Control block known as a loop which you can optimize by:

1. Clicking on the Control category in the blocks palette which is colour-coded gold.

2. Select the `forever` block.

3. Click and drag this into the scripts area, then

4. Drop it underneath the `when clicked` block and above the first `move 10 steps` block.

Once this is done, the C-shaped forever block automatically surrounds the other blocks in your sequence.

The next time you click the green flag, the `forever` block will run over and over again in what is known as an infinite loop in programming.

If you find the sound of constant meowing a bit jarring on your nerves, you can correct that by,

1. Clicking the red octagon next to the green flag above the stage area to stop your program.

2. Change the loop type by clicking and dragging the first `move 10 steps` block.

3. Pull it and the blocks beneath it out of the `forever` block.

4. Drop them underneath the `when clicked` block.

5. Click and drag the `forever` block to the blocks palette to delete it,

6. Click and drag the `repeat 10` block under the `when clicked` block so it goes around the other blocks.

7. Click the green flag to run your new program. Instead of the sequence of instructions running over and over again, the loop ends after ten repetitions. This version is known as a definite loop since you define when it ends.

Most programs like games and sensing programs deploy both definite and infinite loops because they are powerful tools that are key to the operations of programs.

Variables and Conditionals

You will need to master the concepts of variables and conditionals before you can become adept at coding Scratch programs. Like the name suggests, variables refer to values which may vary over time while being run by the program.

Variables have two main properties; a name and its value which doesn't have to be a number. Said value may consist of numbers, text, true-or-false, or might be completely empty (this is known as a null value).

Variables are very important tools. Here's an illustration of how important they are in the context of a game.

The health of a character; the speed of moving objects; the level currently being played and the score are all tracked as variables. Here's how you manage your variables,

1. Click the File menu and save your existing program by clicking on the Save Project.

2. The next step is to click on "File" and "New" start a new, blank project.

3. You then click on the Data category in the blocks palette, then the 'Make a Variable' button.

4. Then type 'loops' as the variable name

5. Continue by clicking the OK button to make a series of blocks appear in the blocks palette.

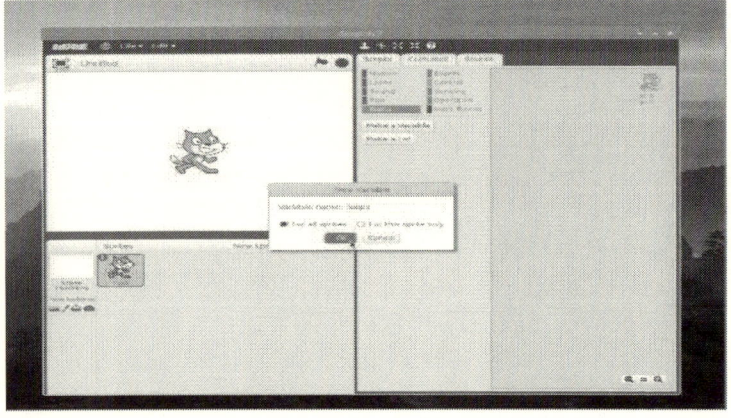

6. Next, you click and drag the `set loops to 0` block to the scripts area. This prompts the program to prime the variable with a value of 0.

7. Click on the "Looks" category of the blocks palette and drag the `say Hello!` block under your `set loops to` block.

The `say Hello!` blocks cause the sprite to describe what is written in them. You could use a variable instead of writing the message in the block. Here's how,

1. Click on the Data category in the blocks palette

2. Click and drag the rounded `loops` block that can be found at the top of the list over the word 'Hello!' in your `say Hello! for 2 secs` block. What you get after this action is a combined block: `say loops for 2 secs`.

3. The next thing you should do is to click on the "Events" category in the blocks palette

4. Then you should click and drag the `when clicked` block so that you can place it at the top of the block sequence.

5. When you click on the green flag above the stage area, the sprite (cat) should say '0' which is the value given to the variable "loops". Check see diagram below

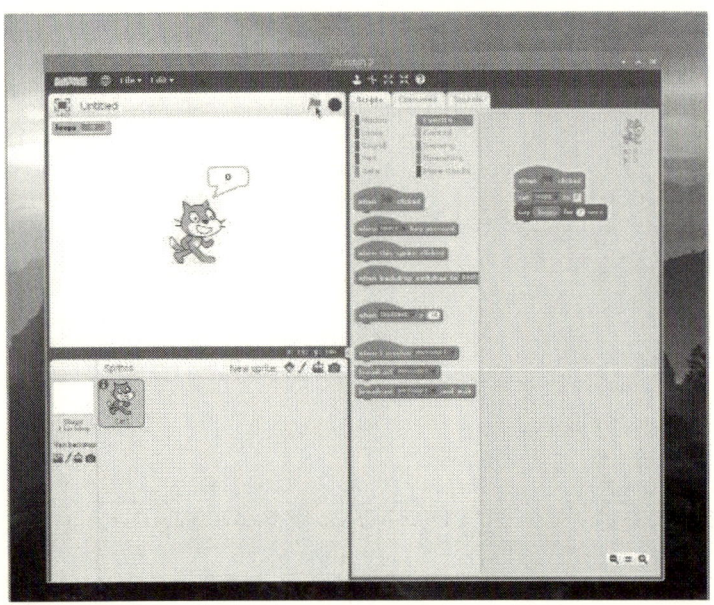

This time the cat will say the value of the variable

But the thing is variables are in a constant state of change. That's what they do. Work on this by,

1. Clicking on the 'Data' category in the blocks palette

2. You should then click and drag the change loops by 1 block to the bottom of your sequence.

3. Right after that, click on the "Control" category,

4. Then click, drag and drop a repeat 10 block directly beneath your set loops to 0 block. It should wrap around the remaining blocks in your sequence.

5. Click the green flag again and note what happens. The sprite (cat) should count upwards from 0 to 9. This happens because your program is in the process of modifying itself. What this means is that for every time the loop runs, the value in the 'loops' variable is increased by the program.

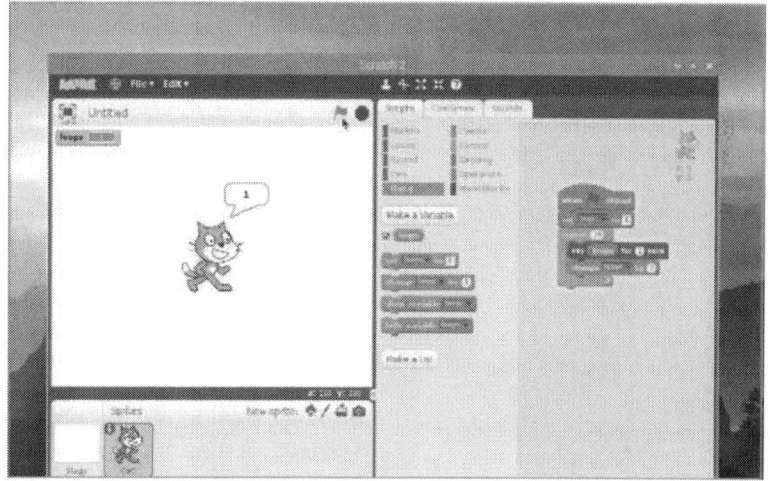

Thanks to the loop, the cat now counts upwards

Counting From Zero

Did you notice that although the sprite only counts to nine, your loop runs ten times? This reason is that you started with a value of zero for the variable. When you include zero and nine, you will find that there are ten numbers between zero and nine.

This is why the program always stops before the cat gets to '10'. You can change this by setting the variable's initial value at 1 instead of 0. But then, modifying a variable is just one of the many things you could do with a variable:

1. Click and drag the `say loops for 2 secs` block so you break it out of the `repeat 10` block after which you drop it below `repeat 10` block.

2. Click and drag the repeat 10 block to the blocks palette to delete it after which you replace it with `a repeat until` block. Ensure that the block is connected to the bottom of the `say loops for 2 secs` block while surrounding the other blocks in your sequence.

3. Go to the "Operators" category in the blocks palette which is color-coded green

4. Click and drag the diamond-shaped n = n block

5. Then drop it on the matching diamond-shaped hole in the `repeat until` block.

The "Operators" block allows the comparison of two values, including variables.

1. Click on the "Data" category in the blocks palette

2. Drag the loops reporter block into the first empty square in the = Operators block

3. Then click on the second empty square before typing the number '10'.

4. When you click on the green flag above the stage area, the sprite should count from 0 up to 9 before the program stops.

This happens as a result of the repeat until block working in a similar way to the repeat 10 block. However, the difference is that instead of totaling the number of loops itself, it compares the value of the 'loops' variable to the value typed to the right of the block. That is why the program stops when the 'loops' variable reaches 10.

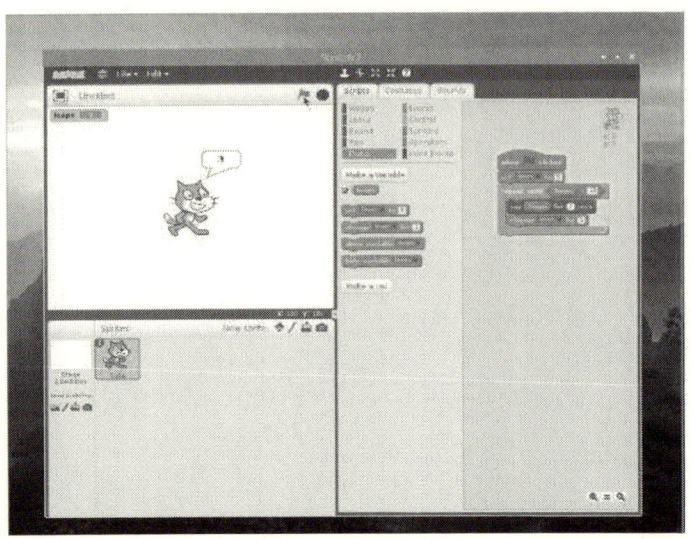

Using a 'repeat until' block with a comparative operator

In programming, this is known as a comparative operator because its operations involve comparing two values.

1. Click on the "Operators" category of the blocks palette where you should find the two other diamond-shape blocks above and below the one with the '=' symbol. There are two comparative operators. The first is the '<' operator which compares two values and is triggered when the value of the left is smaller while the '>' is triggered when the value on the left is bigger.

2. Click on the Control category of the blocks palette where you will find the if then block

3. You then click and drag it to the scripts area

4. Drop it directly beneath the say loops for 2 secs block where it should automatically surround the change loops by 1 block

5. You then click and drag on the block in order to move up to the point where it connects to the bottom of the if then block.

6. Click on the "Looks" category of the blocks palette

7. You should then click and drag a say Hello! block for 2 secs

8. Then you drop the block inside the if then block.

9. After that, click on the "Operators" category of the blocks palette,

10. The next step is to click and drag the n > n block into the diamond-shape hole in your if then block.

Note that if the block is a conditional block. This means that the blocks inside it will only run when you meet certain conditions.

11. Click on the "Data" category of the blocks palette

12. After which you drag and drop the loops reporter block into the first empty square in the `> n` block

13. You should then click on the second empty square after which you type the number '5'.

14. The last but not the final step is to click on the word 'Hello!' in your `say Hello! for 2 secs` block and type 'That's high!'.

When you click on the green flag there might not be obvious changes to the program as you might observe the sprite counting upwards from zero. Note that after it gets to 6 which is the first number greater than 5, the if then block begins to trigger. Consequently, the sprite comments on how high the numbers are getting.

You deserve accolades at this point because you have now gotten the skills to work with variables and conditionals!

The cat makes a comment when the number reaches 6

CHALLENGE: HIGH AND LOW

So here is a quick question, how do you change the program so that the sprite comments on the numbers below 5? Is there a way to make the sprite comment on both high and low numbers? You might want to experiment with the if then else block to make life easier for you.

Chapter 13: Your first Scratch Project— Astronaut Reaction Timer

By now you should have an understanding of how Scratch works. This is the point where you get slightly more interactive. Try the reaction timer which was designed to honor Tim Peake, a British ESA astronaut who spent a significant amount of time aboard the International Space Station.

So your best bet would be to save your existing program. But you could keep it by opening a new project by;

1. Clicking on "File" and "New". But you should give the project a new name by clicking on "File" and "Save" Project. You may choose to call it 'Astronaut Reaction Timer'.

The project relies on a stage background and a sprite. Incidentally, both are not included in Scratch's built-in resources. So if you choose to download them;

1. Click on the raspberry icon so that you can load the Raspbian menu

2. Then you move the mouse pointer to "Internet", after which

3. Click on the Chromium Web Browser. When the browser loads, type rpf.io/astronaut-backdrop into the address bar after which you click on the ENTER key.

4. You should then "right-click" on the picture of space and,

5. Then you click on 'Save image as...', after which

6. You should go on to choose the "Downloads" folder after which,

7. Clicking on the "Save" button should be the next step.

8. After step 7, click on the address bar where you type rpf.io/astronaut-sprite after which, you click on the ENTER key.

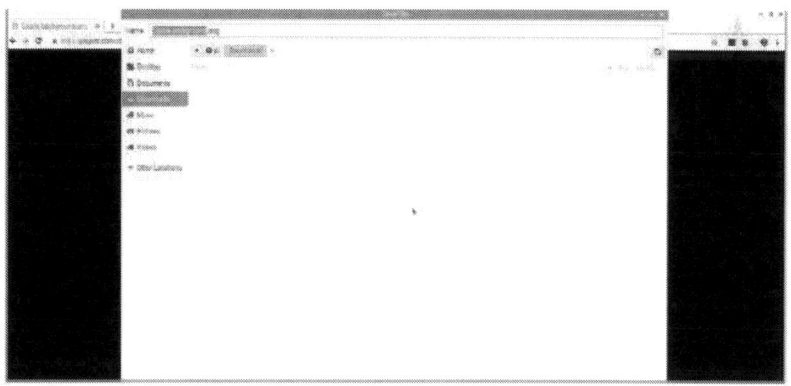

Save the background image

After all the above, your next step should be to right-click on the picture of Tim Peake. After that,

1. Click on 'Save image as...',

2. After which you choose the "Downloads" folder

3. Then click on the "Save" button. After saving both images, you may close Chromium (optional) before using the taskbar to revert to Scratch 2 or 3.

USER INTERFACE

Having gotten to this point, you should be familiar with the Scratch 2 or 3 user interface (assuming you started the guidelines from the start of the chapter).

The next instructions are based on your familiarity with the program. In case you get lost, you may want to go back to the picture of the user interface at the start of the chapter. Hopefully you will get a reminder. That said,

1. Right-click the sprite on the stage, then select "Delete".

2. Next, you should find the stage controls at the left(bottom) of the Scratch window,

3. After which you click on the upload backdrop icon.

4. Look for the file "Space-background.png". It should be in the "Downloads" folder,

5. After finding it, click to select it, after which you click "OK". All things being equal, there should be a picture of space instead of a plain white stage background.

The scripts area should also be replaced by the backdrops area. Although you should be able to draw over the backdrop, in the meantime you should simply click on the tab marked "Scripts" which can be found at the top of the Scratch 2 window.

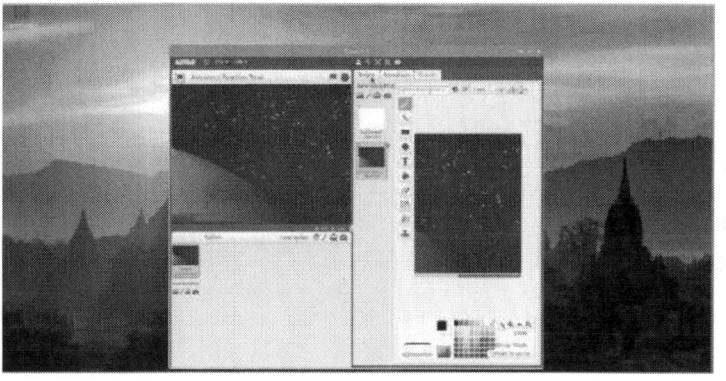

The space background appears on the stage

After doing all of the above, you can upload your new sprite by

1. Clicking the upload sprite icon which is next to the words 'New sprite that should be right at the top of the sprites pane.

2. Select a certain file labeled "Astronaut-Tim.png" which should be in the Downloads folder,

3. You should then select it by clicking OK. This will make the sprite to automatically appear on the stage, although it might not be where you want it to be.

4. Correct this by clicking, dragging and dropping it where you want it (lower middle).

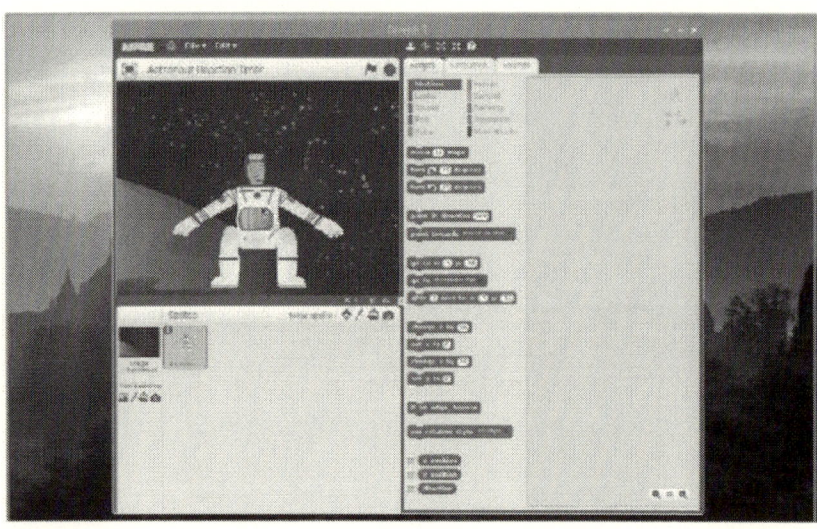

Drag the astronaut sprite to the lower middle of the stage

Now that you have a new background and sprite, creating your program should be a natural step.

1. You might want to start by creating a new variable called 'time'. You should ensure that you select 'For all sprites' before you click OK.

You should then click on your sprite which might be on the stage or in the sprite pane. Do this by,

1. Adding a when clicked block from the "Events" category to the scripts area.

2. Your next step should be to add a say Hello! for 2 secs block from the "Looks" category

3. Click on the block to alter it say 'Hello! British ESA Astronaut Tim Peake here.

4. You then add a wait 1 secs block from the Control category and a say Hello! block.

5. Convert this block to say 'Hit Space!

6. Add a reset timer block from the "Sensing" category. It is used to gauge your reaction to the game because of a unique Scratch variable that is designed to scale time.

7. Your next step would be to add a wait until Control block

8. After which you drag a key space pressed and Sensing block into its white space. This action will bring about a pause in the program that you could end by pressing the SPACE key on the keyboard. Note that the timer would estimate how long it took you to hit the SPACE key after you got the 'Hit Space!' message. To find out how long it took, you would need Time . Ultimately, you would need a join Operators block that makes a concatenation by joining two values (and possibly) variables.

1. The best way around it is to start with a say Hello! block

2. Drag and drop a join Operators block over the word 'Hello!'.

3. Then fill in the first box with 'Your reaction time was '

4. Ensure that you add a blank space at the end,

5. After which, drag another join block into the second box.

6. Then drag a timer reporting block from the Sensing category into the middle box,

7. Type ' seconds' into the last box but be sure to start with a blank space.

8. The last step is to drag a set time to 0 Data variables block to the end of the sequence.

9. Replace the '0' with a timer reporting block and get ready to test your game. After clicking on the green flag above the stage, be prepared to press the SPACE key once you get 'Hit Space!' message.

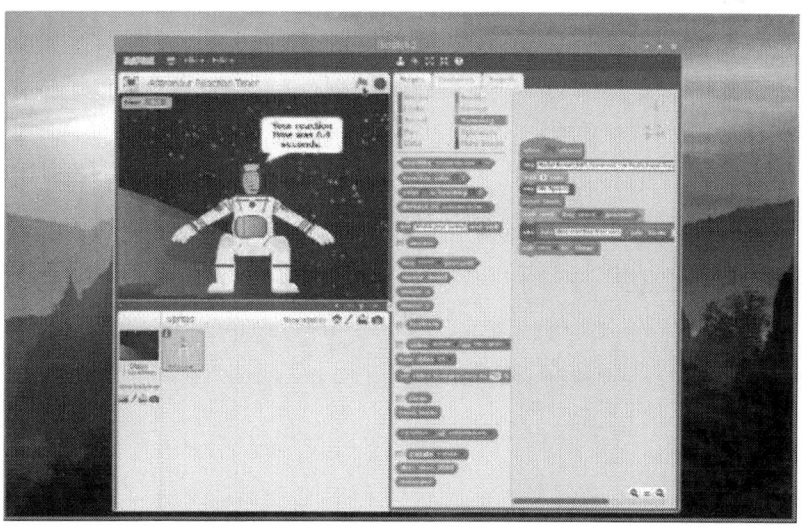

You could further test the strengths of the project by estimating the distance covered by the International Space Station within the period it took you to press the SPACE key.

It is easy since you already have a value which is the station's published speed (seven kilometres per second).

To do this,

1. Create a new variable called 'distance'. You might want to note the way the blocks in the "Data" category spontaneously modify themselves to show the new variable except that program's time variable blocks stay the same.

2. You then add a set distance to 0 block, then drag a ● * ● Operator block(which indicate multiplication)over the '0'.

3. Then drag a time reporting block across the first blank space

4. Type in the number '7' into the second space. After these steps, your combined block should read set distance to time * 7 .This means that the time it took you to press the SPACE key would be multiplied by seven, before the distance traveled by the ISS can be ascertained.

5. Next, you add a wait 1 secs block and change it to '4 secs'.

6. Drag another say Hello! block to the end of your sequence after which you add join blocks like before.

7. Type 'In that time the ISS travels around 'in the first white space. Do not forget to include the space at the end and,

8. Type "kilometres" in the last white space bearing in mind, the space at the start.

9. Drag a round Operators block into the middle blank space

10. You can use a distance reporting block to cover the new blank space by dragging the block. The round block roundup numbers to the nearest whole number. This means the results are easy to read instead of figures that are difficult to read.

11. Click the green flag to run your program. You should discover how far the ISS traveled in the time it takes to hit the SPACE key. Do not forget to save your program after you are done. This makes it easy for you to load it again in the future.

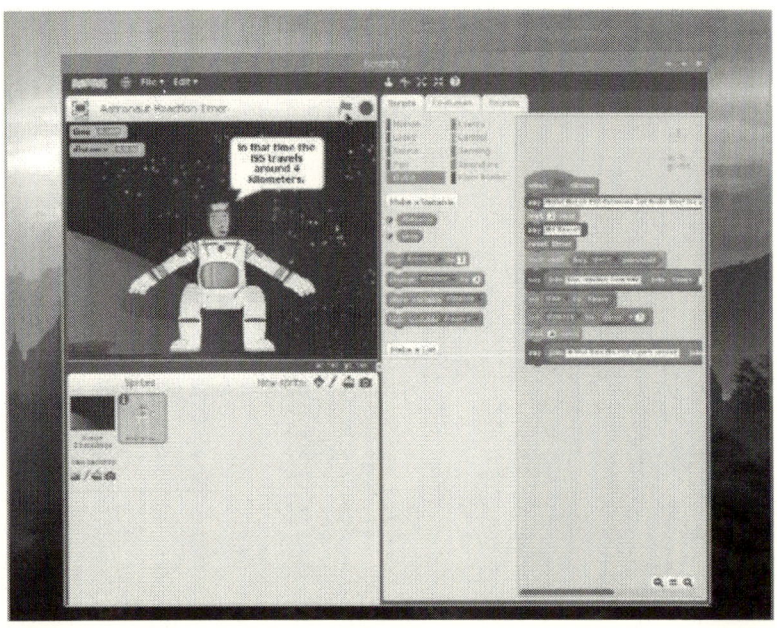

CHALLENGE: WHO'S FAST?

Apart from space travel, which other professions require split-second reflexes? Is it possible to draw your own sprites and backgrounds to show at least one of these professions?

Chapter 14: Second Scratch Project— Synchronised Swimming

This project shows how most games use two-button control by demonstrating the use of the ← and → keys on the keyboard.

1. Start by creating a new project which you should save as 'Synchronised Swimming'.

2. Click on the Stage in the stage control section

3. You then click the Backdrops tab.

4. Click on a water-like blue color from the palette

5. Then click on the fill with color icon after which,

6. You click on the white backdrop

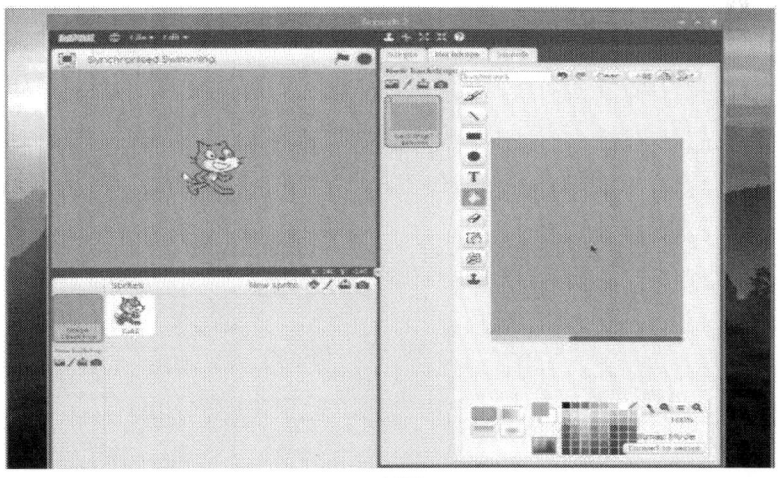

: Fill the background with a blue colour

7. Right-click the sprite

8. Then click 'delete'.

9. Go to the sprite area where you click the 'choose sprite from library' icon. You should find a list of built-in sprites.

10. Then you click on the "Animals" category

11. Select 'Cat1 Flying' then click OK. This sprite should suit swimming projects.

12. Click the new sprite

13. You then drag the two when space key pressed events blocks into the scripts area.

14. Next you click on the small down-arrow next to the word 'space' on the first block before choosing 'left arrow' from the possible options.

15. Drag a turn 15 degrees Motion block under your when left arrow pressed block, before doing the same with your second Events block. The only difference is that you should choose 'right arrow' from the list using a turn 15 degree a Motion block.

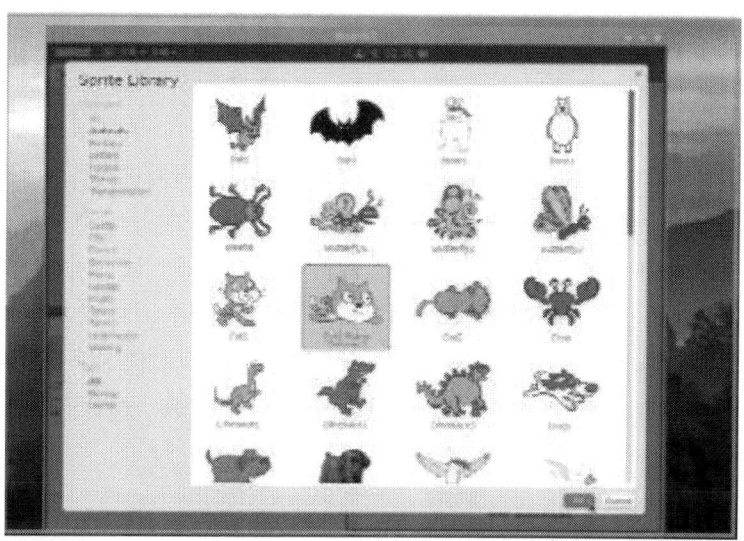

Test your program by pressing either of the ← or → keys. Notice how the sprite turns in line with the key you press. The Events trigger blocks, you previously selected are constantly active even when the program isn't 'running'. So there is no need to click on the green flag.

You should repeat the steps twice but this time choose 'up arrow' and 'down arrow' for the Events trigger blocks.

Do the same for the move 10 steps and move -10 steps for the Motion blocks.

After executing these steps, watch how the sprite turns around and swims in different directions when you press the arrow keys.

You could make the sprite's movements better. You could also change what is known as Scratch speak as its costumes (appearance).

Here's how,

1. First click on the sprite,

2. Next, you click on the "Costumes" tab above the blocks palette.

3. Then click on the 'cat1 flying-a' costume

4. Select the round X icon that appears at its top-right corner to delete it.

Then you click on the 'cat1 flying-b' costume after which you rename it using the name box at the top. (see Figure 4-17).

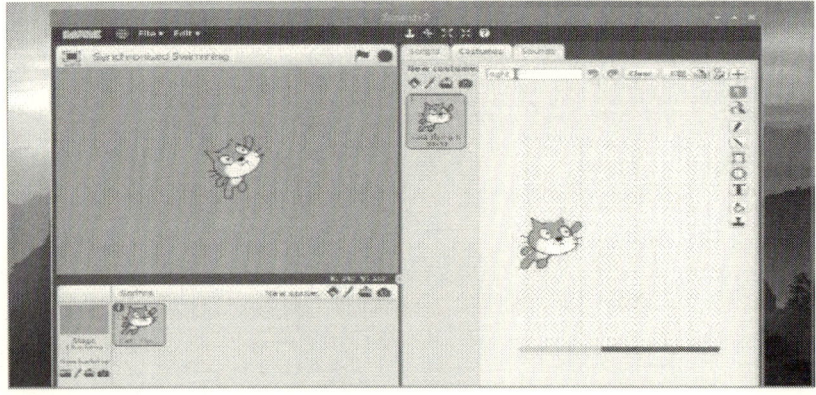

Rename the costume as 'right'

5. You then right-click on the renamed costume

6 .Click 'duplicate' to create a copy

7. Select this copy before clicking on the flip left-right icon. You can then rename.

Follow the steps above and you will be able to get two replica 'costumes' for your sprite. Both of which will match the direction that the sprite faces.

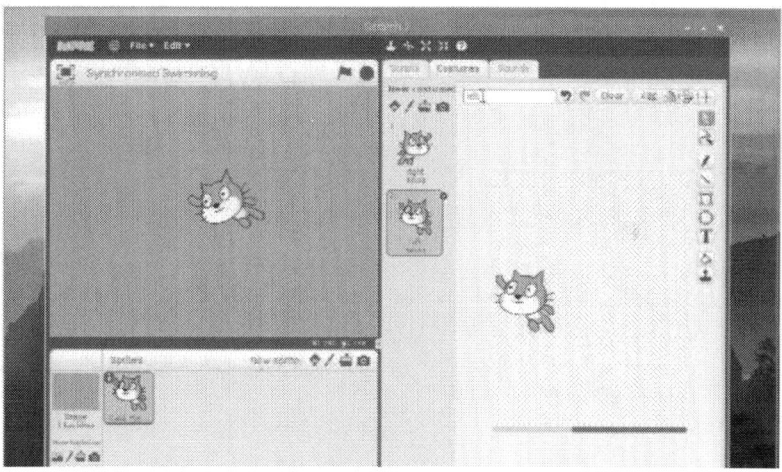

Select the Scripts tab above the costume area after which drag two switch costumes to the left. Then look at the blocks under your left arrow and right arrow Events blocks.

Do not change block under the right arrow block to read switch costume to right and watch how the sprite seems to face different directions when swimming.

The demands for Olympic-style synchronised swimming make it imperative that the sprite's position be reset. Here's how you go about it

1. Start by adding a when clicked Events block,

2. Add a go to x: 0 y: 0 Motion block (you might need to change values)and a point in direction 90 Looks block underneath.

3. Here's the time to click the green flag. Watch how the sprite moves to the middle of the stage while pointing to the right.

Should you choose to create more swimmers, here's how to go about it

1. Start by adding a repeat 6 block (you might want to change the default value of '10') which should include a create clone of myself Control block inside. Prevent the swimmers from swimming in the same direction by,

2. Adding a turn 60 degrees block above the create clone block which should be inside the repeat 6 block.

3. Click the green flag then press the arrow keys and watch how animated the swimmers become.

What about some music to make things more realistic? To achieve this, follow these steps,

1. Click on the Sounds tab above the blocks palette

2. Select the 'choose new sound from library' icon.

3. Then click on the Music Loops category

4. Proceed to select the music of your choice by clicking on the small play icons.

5. Make your choice by clicking on the "OK" button

6. Then click on the "Scripts" tab to open the scripts area again.

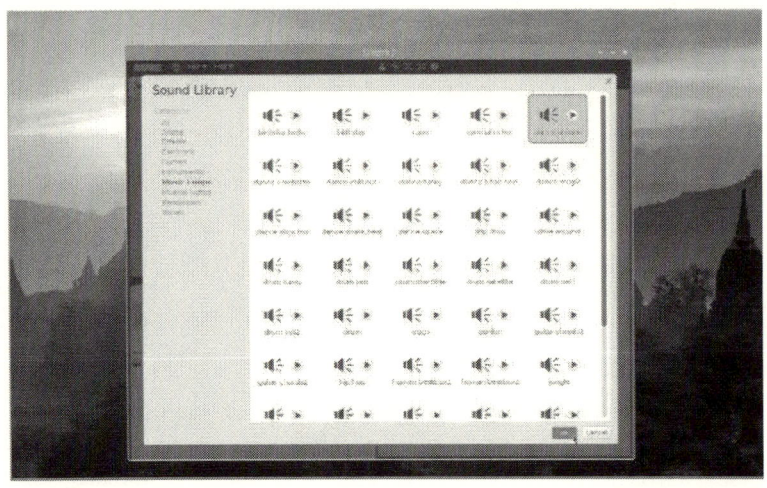

Select a music loop from the sound library

1. Add another when clicked Events block to the scripts area.

2. Go on to add a forever Control block.

3. Add a play sound dance around until done block to the Control block. After selecting music of your choice, test your program by clicking the green flag. If you choose to stop the music just click on the red octagon.

Lastly, do you know that adding a new event trigger will enable you to initiate a full dancing routine?

Follow these steps

1. Start by adding a when space key pressed Events block

2. You should then add a switch costume to right block underneath which you add a repeat 36 block, a turn 10 degrees block and a move 10 steps block. The caveat is that you must change the default value.

3. After clicking on the green flag to start the program, try out the new routine by pressing the SPACE key(see image below). As always, save your program when you're finished.

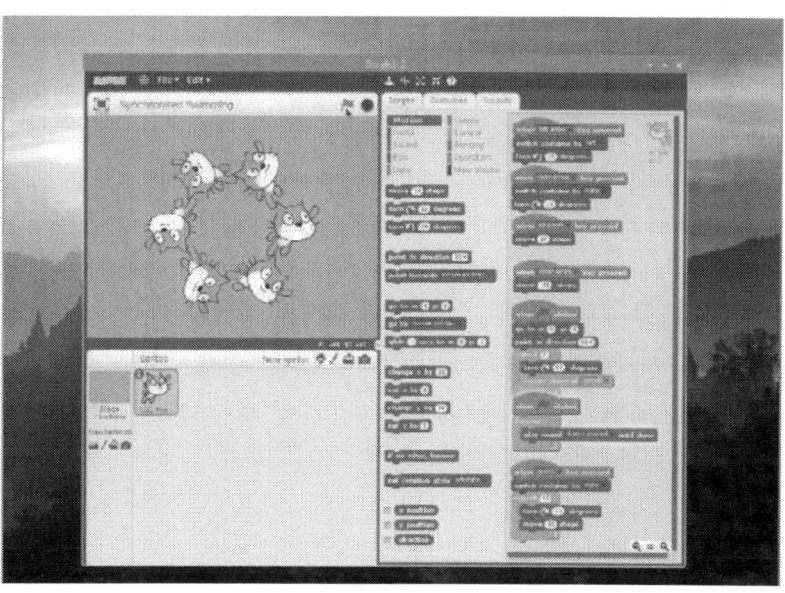

Chapter 15: Project 2: Archery Game

By now you should have some mastery of Scratch .This means that handling advanced tasks like an archery game shouldn't be impossible for you to handle..

1. Open the Chrome Web Browser and type rpf.io/archery-resources

2. Press the ENTER key and hopefully, it should take a few seconds for the resources of the game to download.

3. Switch to Scratch 2

4. Click on the File menu then "Load Project'.

5. Select 'pi' in the Places pane at the left-hand side of the window after which you click on the 'Downloads' folder

6. Click on ArcheryResources.sb2 first and the "Open button" next to it. At this point, you will have the option of replacing the contents of your current project. So if you haven't saved your changes, now is the time to click on "Cancel" to save them if you want to. If not, simply click OK.

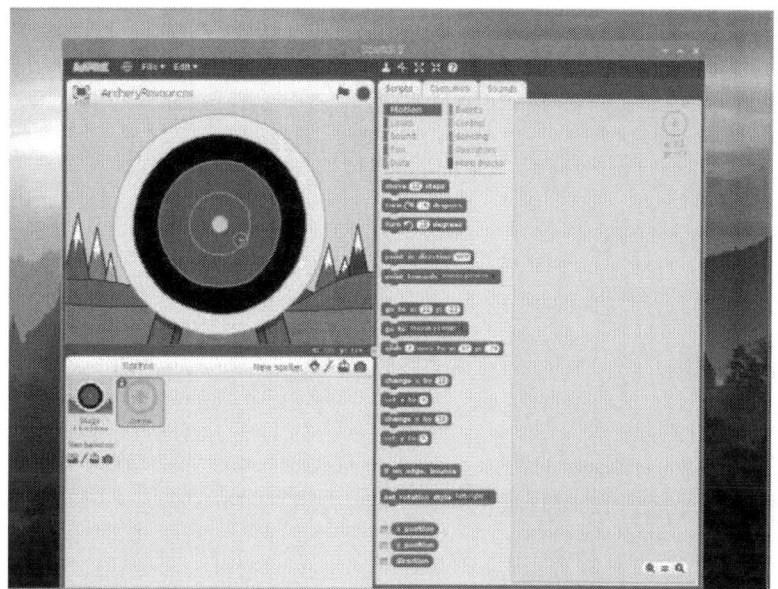

Resources project loaded for the archery game

Although the project you just loaded has a backdrop and a sprite and it does not have the code that you need to make a game. You have to add that:

1. Start by adding a when clicked block,

2. Then proceed to a broadcast message1 block.

3. Click on the down arrow at the end of the block to select 'New Message'

4. Type in 'new arrow' before clicking the on "OK" button. Your block should now read broadcast new arrow.

Broadcasts are simply messages between the different parts of your program. To optimize your broadcasts,

1. Add when I receive message1 block then modify it to read when I receive new arrow. Simply click on the down arrow and select 'new arrow' from the list. This action prevents you from repeating the message.

2. Just underneath your when I receive new arrow block, do add a go to x: -150 y: -150 block and a set size to 400 % block. However, be sure to change the values for those blocks once they have been dragged down to the scripts area.

3. Click on the green flag. The arrow sprite which is used to aim at the target should jump to the bottom-left of the stage and become four times its size.

Make things more interesting and challenging for the player, by

1. Adding movements that simulate swaying while the archer takes aim.

2. Drag a forever block, followed by glide 1 secs to x: -150 y: -150 block.

3. Edit the first white box to say '0.5' instead of '1,'

4. After that, put a pick random -150 to 150 Operators block in each of the other two white boxes. This causes the arrow to drift around the stage randomly, thus, making it difficult to hit the target.

5. Click the green flag again. Note how your sprite drifts around the stage while it covers different parts of the target. The issue at the moment is that you cannot shoot at the target. To do this,

1. Drag a when space key pressed block into your scripts area

2. Follow up with a stop all Control block.

3. Then click on the down arrow at the end of the block before modifying it to a stop other scripts in sprite block.

If you have to stop your program in the course of adding new blocks, just press the SPACE key after clicking on the green flag to restart it. The sprite should be moving although you will need to make the arrow's flight more realistic.

1. Add a repeat 50 block followed by a change size by -10 block

2. Click the green flag to test your game and watch the arrow fly away from your route to the target.

Keeping score makes the game more interesting. Here's how

1. Add an if then block (but ensure that it's under the repeat 50 block) to a touching color? Choose the kind of color you want by

2. Clicking on the colored box at the end of the Sensing block

3. You then click on the yellow bull's-eye of your target on the stage.

How does the player know when they have scored?

1. Add a play sound cheer block and a say 200 points for 2 secs block inside the if then block.

To rearm the player

1. Add a broadcast new arrow block to the very bottom of the block stack, just below and outside the if then block.

2. Click the green flag to start your game. Attempt hitting the bull's-eye and get a cheer from the crowd whenever you do, in addition to a 200-point score!

At this point we could say that the game is a success although there is room for improvement. Based on what you have learnt in this chapter, keep improving on it. Try adding scores for hitting parts of the target other than the bull's-eye. You could make it more interesting by recording corresponding points to the areas hit. Say 100 points for red, 50 points for blue etc.

Chapter 16: Programming With Python

Python, a word that is now associated with computer programming was coined from the Monty Python comedy troupe. Python is among the favorite programming languages, used to create dynamic applications and solutions around the world. It is not a visual environment common with Scratch. You will find Python's text based simulation handful and practical.

The text based layout allows you to write instructions with a specific language and syntax which your computer interprets.

If you have dabbled with Scratch for some time, Python is a great next step for you since it offers you increased flexibility where you enjoy a traditional programming adventure.

At this point, you might be thinking that it is difficult to learn, it is not. With practice, you can start writing simple programs like basic calculations. When your confidence is high, and you have mastered this programming language, you can start designing applications like complex games and 3D environments.

In this chapter, you will understand the terminology and concepts introduced in the previous chapter.

Introducing the Thonny Python IDE

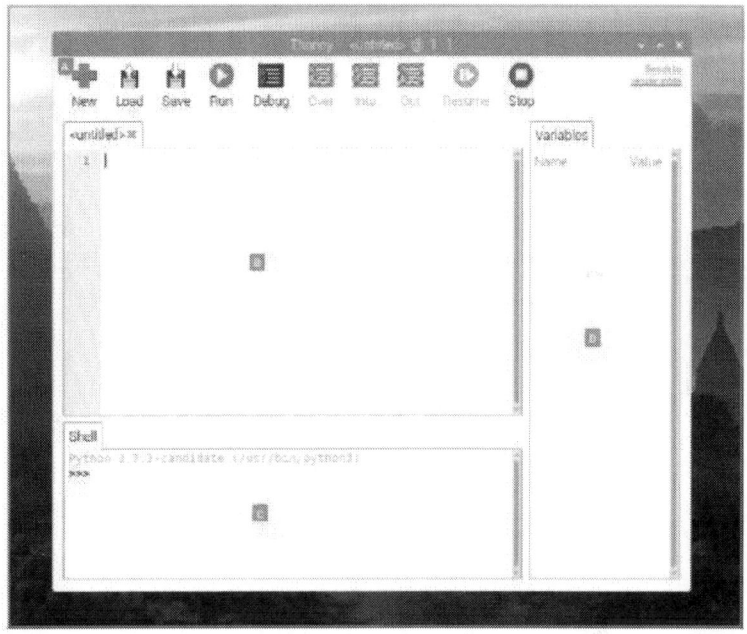

Toolbar— the simple mode module of Thonny Python comes with attractive icons on its menu bar. The icons are pretty straightforward, representing different functions that allow you to save, create, load, and run your programs in various ways. Script area—your python programs are implemented at the script area which is usually split into two-major and supplementary.

The major area takes the bulk of space, serving as a canvass for your programs including a complementary side margin that displays line numbers.

Python shell—running your codes are usually done here as well as options about how your programs should run.

In addition, you can input individual instructions that are quickly implemented as soon as you press the ENTER key.

Variable area—for convenience and easy tracking, all changes–either intentional or unintentional are accessible in this section. Think of this area as a log of your sessions when you create and run programs.

YOUR FIRST PYTHON Program: Hello, World!

If you want to access Thonny from the menu, you should go to its icon directly. Just like other pre-installed applications on the Raspberry Pi, Thonny is quite visible with its unique icon. Click on the Raspberry icon, move the cursor to the programming section, and click on Thonny Python IDE. Wait for a few seconds as the program—usually the simple mode loads, welcoming your eyes to its user interface.

Basically, Thonny is an integrated development environment (IDE). And what it does is to bring together the tools that are required to design, write or develop software into a holistic user-interface experience. Think of Thonny as a hybrid with a capability for supporting one programming language unlike others that clearly supports various languages.

The biggest takeaway from using Python is the absence of visual feedback as you create programs unlike Scratch with real-time graphics.

You will enjoy this traditional programming language of hard line codes better than modern iterations available on other IDEs. To start your first program, click on the Python shell area at the bottom-left of the Thonny window; type this instruction and press ENTER:

> print("Hello, World!")

After hitting the ENTER key, your program runs instantly. When you see 'Hello, World!' your program was run successfully. In addition, your program runs immediately in the shell area because the interpreter clearly examined your codes and instructions, found it valid and interpreted it. The whole parsing process that is displayed in the shell area is known as the interactive mode, more like a face-to-face interaction with your friend where communication is enriched by sending, processing and receiving information.

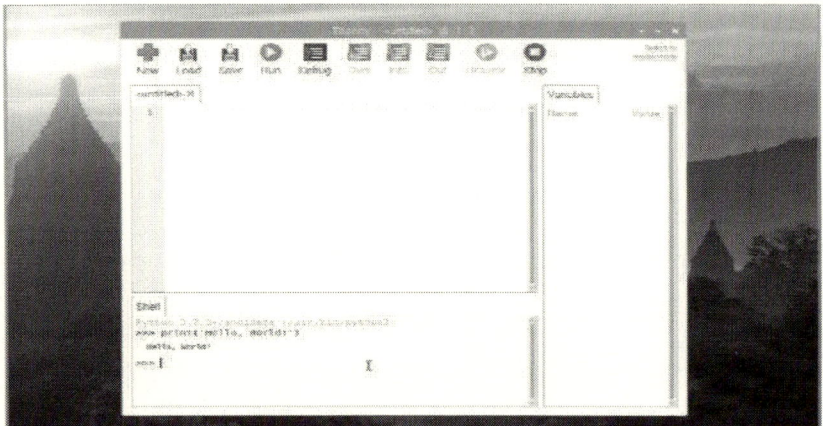

Hello World!

Syntax error

Coding is interesting when your programs are implemented just the way you created it. It can be frustrating when you cannot fathom the incidents that surround a 'syntax error' message. Usually, a syntax error message is displayed at the shell area which means that your codes are not properly written.

Remember that when you omit a bracket and a quotation mark, or misspelled 'print' with extra symbols; your program will not run. To salvage the situation, type the instruction again, and ensure that the codes are an exact replica of the example provided in this book. Then press the ENTER key.

Click on the script area at the left-hand side of the Thonny window and type your program again.

    print("Hello, World!")

After you click the ENTER key, there are no changes except a visible blank line in the script area. If you want to try this out, click the Run icon on the Thonny toolbar. A prompt appears immediately, asking you to save your session.

Use a descriptive name like "Hello World" while using the save button. When your program has been stored on your system, two messages appear in the shell area.

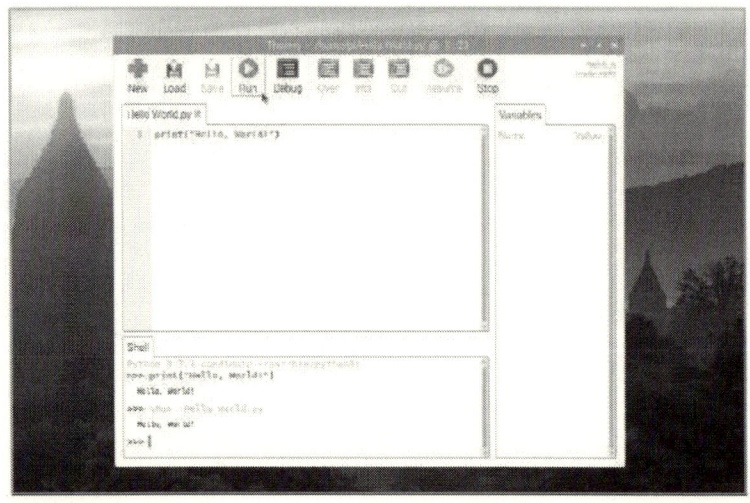

While the first message is clearly a command from Thonny, asking the interpreter to load the program you just saved; the other one is an output of the program.

Congratulations!

You can call yourself a coder as you have executed your first program using interactive and script models.

Challenge: New message

Now that you can run programs using interactive and script methods, you may face some difficulties changing the message executed by the Python program.

In addition, you may be confused when choosing the best method to support the addition of new messages and perhaps you wonder what happens when you remove the brackets or quotation marks from the codes and consequently run it.

Next Steps: Loops and Code Indentation

Python controls how functions and strings are arranged and connected with a technology known as indentation. This system ensures that your programs are interpreted smoothly.

Create a new program by clicking on New icon in the Thonny toolbar. A new tab is created just above the former one where you can run new programs while working on the other program. You may commence with the following instruction:

> print("Loop starting!") for i in range (10):

What you see on the first line as an output in the shell area resembles the earlier feedback from the Hello world program.

The second output kick-start a definite loop, similar to Scratch where (I) is assigned to the loop with a series of numbers. The numbers in the loop begin at 0 oscillating between 0 and 10 but never quite reaching 10. The colon symbol (:) means that subsequent instruction after the symbol is invalid and will not be parsed by the interpreter.

Recall that in Scratch, the instructions contained in the loop was embedded in the C-shaped pattern of connection, informing the syntax and how the programs are interpreted. Python has a similar function too, utilizing a different method evident with indenting codes.

Indenting your code on python is present by default and makes your lines clear with serial numbers attached to each instruction. Failure to implement and understand this concept leaves you with blank spaces and a headache.

CHALLENGE: ALTER THE LOOK

To create content that engages your end users, employ images to create fun just like other popular culture with Halloween costume. Here, you will create a prank using colors and image where you create a wonderful experience with a picture.

You can go about this by drawing your own spot-the-difference and scary images (using a graphics editor such as GIMP). Similarly, you could also raise the credibility of this challenge, putting in place tracking measures to ascertain users who correctly spotted the difference.

Chapter 17: Your First Python Projects— Turtle Snowflakes

Now that you understand how Python works, it's time to infuse graphics and create a snowflake using a tool known as a turtle.

Physical robots imitate the natural order of things in the environment, especially animals. A turtle in the wild just like its digital companion moves in a straight line, make turns, with minimal limb coordination.

Think of that motion on your screen where the turtle draws a line from a point to another. Unlike some other languages, namely Logo and its many variants, Python doesn't have a turtle tool built into it. However, a huge library of add-on codes allows the motion of the turtle to be quite practical.

Libraries are arrays of code that adds new instructions and variables stretching Python's realm of possibilities further. Using an import command, you can start creating awesome content with this skill.

To create a new program to test your skill in this area, click on the New icon, and type the following: import turtle

When you use a data from a library, it is expedient that you use the name of the data followed by a syntax arrangement.

You are required to use the library name followed by a full stop, and then the instruction follows.

That can be annoying to type out every time, so you can assign a shorter variable name instead –preferably one letter which doubles as a pet name for the turtle. Type the following:

    pat = turtle.Turtle()

To test your program out, you'll need to give your turtle something to do. Type:

    pat.forward(100)

Click the Run icon, and save your program as Turtle Snowflakes. After doing this, a new window called 'Turtle Graphics' will appear where you get a taste of your program: your turtle, Pat, will move forwards 100 units, drawing a straight line.

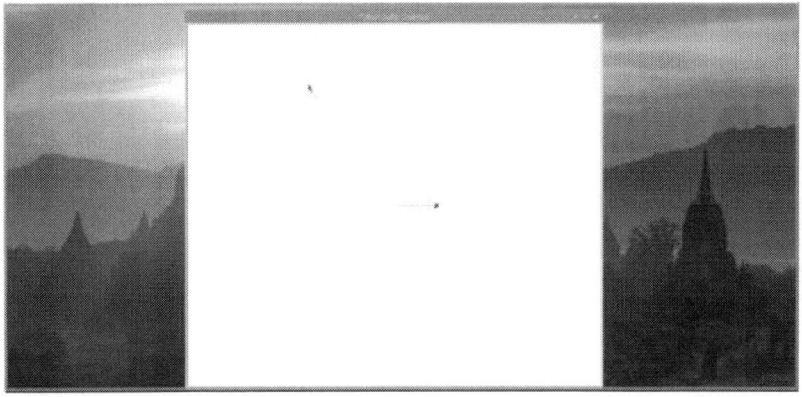

Matt drawing a line!

When switching back to the Thonny window from the graphics canvas, you may not easily find it because it is usually at the background. Take your cursor to the minimize function and click it or you move to the task bar directly at the top of the screen where you can also hit the stop button to collapse the Turtle Graphics window.

Typing out every single movement instruction by hand would be tedious, so delete line 3 and create a loop to do the hard work of carving out shapes:

```
for i in range(2):
    pat.forward(100)
    pat.right(60)
    pat.forward(100)
    pat.right(120)
```

Run your program, and Pat will draw a single parallelogram

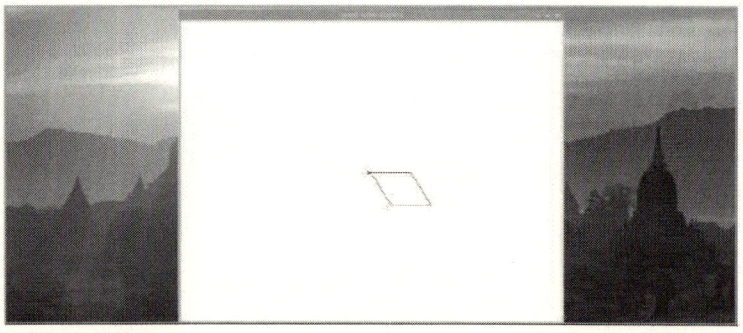

To transform this into a snowflake-like shape, click the Stop icon in the main Thonny window and create a loop around your loop by substituting this instruction in line 3:

```
for i in range(10):
```

...and the following at the bottom of your program:

pat.right(36)

Your program won't run as it is, because the existing loop isn't indented correctly. To fix that, click on the start of each line in the existing loop – line 4 through 8 – and press the SPACE key four times to correct the indentation. Your program should now look like this: import turtle

Click the Run icon, and watch the turtle: it'll draw a parallelogram, as before, but when it's done it'll turn 36 degrees and draw another, then another, and so on until there are ten overlapping parallelograms on the screen – looking a little like a snowflake

While a robotic turtle draws in a single color on a large piece of paper, Python's simulated turtle can use a range of colors.

Add a new line 3 and 4, pushing the existing lines down:

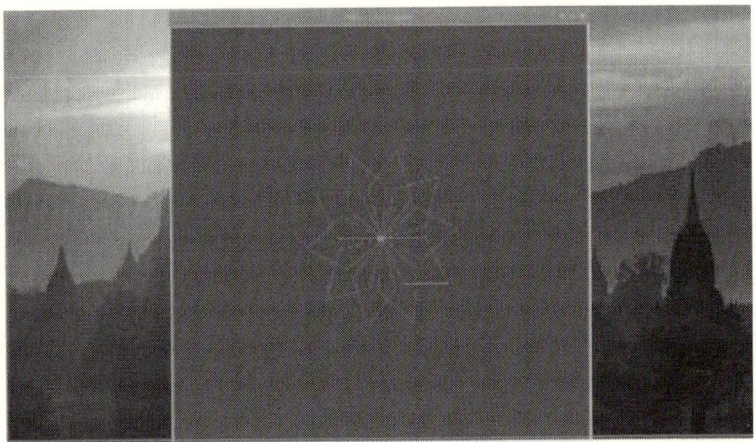

You can also have the colors chosen randomly from a list, using the random library. Go back to the top of your program and insert the following as line 2: import random

In your line 4, change the background color from 'blue' to 'grey', then create a new variable called 'colors' while inserting a new line 5:

> colours = ["cyan", "purple", "white", "blue"]

U.S. SPELLINGS

Many programming languages use American English by default, especially spellings. Python is no exception. The earlier command in line 5 ought to be spelled color rather than color. When you use British spellings, your program will fail to run.

This rule does not overlap to words associated to Variables where you exercise freedom with semantics.

Using the line 5 example again, this type of variable is called a list, and is marked by square brackets where the snowflake appears in specific colors but you still need to tell Python to choose one each time the loop repeats itself. At the very end of the program, enter the following – making sure it's indented with four spaces so it forms part of the outer loop, just like the line above it:

    pat.color(random.choice(colours))

Click the Run icon and the snowflake-stroke-ninja-star will be magically drawn. This time around, Python will choose a random color from your list as it draws each petal – giving the snowflake a pleasing, multicolor finish.

Using random colors for the 'petals'

Now that you can create a ninja star, you should write codes that will bring to life a benign snowflake, which looks closely like real life. To make this happen, add a new line 6 directly below your colors list with the following instruction:

    pat.penup()   pat.forward(90)   pat.left(45) pat.pendown()

The penup and pendown instructions moves a simulated pen off and on the graphics page just like what obtains with a paper surface. Rather than using a loop, like you have been doing, you're going to create a function that can be recalled when you need it. And the function remains in your portfolio.

Start by deleting the code for drawing your parallelogram-based snowflakes: that's everything between and including the pat.color("cyan") instruction on line 10 through to pat.right(36) on line 17.

Don't tamper with pat.color(random.choice(colours)) code but inject a hash symbol (#) at the start of the line. Using a hash creates an emphasis known as commenting which can follow the instructions which Python ignores when interpreting the lines of code. You can also add explanations to your code with comments for clarity where you come back to it after some time or share it.

Function is created by first defining it. Define your function with 'branch', by typing the following instruction in line 10, just below pat.pendown():

    def branch():

This instruction defines your function, using the choice of values you want in the branch container. When you press the ENTER key, Thonny will include an indentation for the function's instructions.

Type the following while paying close attention to indentation because a misplaced blank space would affect your nesting efforts sooner, rather than later.

```
for i in range(3):

    for i in range(3):

        pat.forward(30)

        pat.backward(30)

        pat.right(45)

    pat.left(90)

    pat.backward(30)

    pat.left(45)

    pat.right(90)

    pat.forward(90)
```

Make sure that the new loop you create remains above the commented-out color line.

You should as well run and call your new function:

for i in range(8):

branch()

pat.left(45)

Your finished program should look like this:

```
import turtle
import random
pat = turtle.Turtle()
turtle.Screen().bgcolor("grey")
colours = ["cyan", "purple", "white", "blue"]
pat.penup()
pat.forward(90)
pat.left(45)
pat.pendown()
def branch():
    for i in range(3):
        for i in range(3):
            pat.forward(30)
            pat.backward(30)
            pat.right(45)
        pat.left(90)
        pat.backward(30)
        pat.left(45)
    pat.right(90)
```

> pat.forward(90) for i in range(8):
>
> branch()
>
> pat.left(45)
>
> # pat.color(random.choice(colours))

Click on Run and watch the graphics window as Pat implements your instructions.

Congratulations: your snowflake now looks a lot more like a snowflake than anything else.

Finally! A snowflake to remember.

CHALLENGE: WHAT NEXT?

Can you use your commented-out instruction to have the branches of the snowflake drawn in different colours? Can you create a 'snowflake' function, and use it to draw lots of snowflakes on the screen? Can you have your program change the size and colour of the snowflakes at random?

Chapter 18: Your Second Python Project— Scary Spot the Difference

This project will demonstrate to you the capability of Python to scale pictures and sounds as well as turtle-based graphics, which will be used here as a prank on your friends. This project requires two images–your spot-the-difference image with a 'scary' surprise image and a sound file.

To start, click on the raspberry icon to load the Raspbian menu, choose the Internet category, and click on Chromium Web Browser. When it has loaded, type rpf.io/spot-pic into the address bar followed by the ENTER key.

After you have chosen your preferred picture, Right-click on the picture and click on 'Save image as...', choose the /home/pi folder, then click Save. Click back on Chromium's address bar, then type rpf.io/scary-pic followed by the ENTER key.

As before, right-click the picture, click 'Save image as...', choose the /home/pi folder, then click Save.

For the sound file, you'll need to type rpf.io/scream into the address bar followed by the ENTER key. While it downloads, think of where you will move it to because you may not be able to use it without moving it to an accessible folder.

Click on the raspberry icon, find the Accessories category, and click on File Manager. In the folder list, double-click on Downloads. Find the file scream.wav within this folder, right-click on it, and then click Cut. Click on pi in the folder list to the left, then right-click on a blank space in the main window area before clicking Paste. You can now close the File Manager and Chromium.

After you have moved the image, Click the New icon in the Thonny toolbar to begin a new project. The best way to experience the dynamic use of Python's capabilities is through the appreciation of a resource like Pygame that is created for games. Type the following:

> import pygame

To use data from other libraries, including a part of the Pygame library. Import them by typing the following:

from pygame.locals import * from time import sleep

from random import import randrange

You want to use a specific data from a library rather than the whole bank of data. Thereafter, you create a Pygame setup, which is a concept known as initialisation. In order to improve the validity of the Pygame framework, set the resolution of your TV and monitor.

Type the following:

pygame.init()

width = pygame.display.Info().current_w
height = pygame.display.Info().current_h

The final step in setting Pygame up is to create its window, which Pygame calls a screen. Type the following:

screen = pygame.display.set_mode((width, height))

pygame.quit()

Take note of the blank line in the middle because your program will stay there. For immediate action, click on the Run icon and save your program as Spot the Difference. Pygame will then create a window or a box with a black background that contains the pixel spatial measurements. Conversely, the variables area fill up with unique values that Pygame has automatically created, you can safely ignore these.

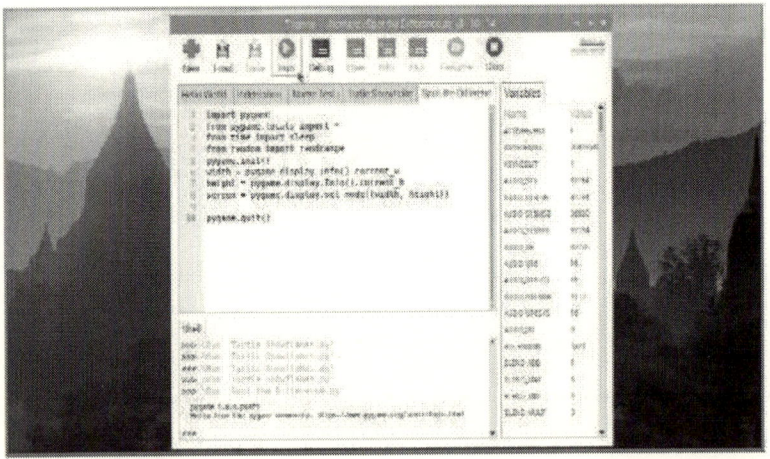

To open and display your desired spot-the-difference image, put the following line in the space above pygame.quit():

difference = pygame.image.load('spot_the_diff.png')

Scale and adjust the width and height of the pixel to make sure the image fills the screen with ease. Then type the following:

> difference = pygame.transform.scale(difference, (width, height))

Now the image is in memory, you need to tell Pygame to actually display it on the screen – a process known as blitting, or a bit block transfer. Type the following:

> screen.blit(difference, (0, 0))
> pygame.display.update()

The first of these lines copies the image onto the screen, starting at the top-left corner; the second tells Pygame to redraw the screen. Without this second line, the image will be in the correct place in memory but you'll never see it!

Click on the Run icon, and the image will briefly appear on screen.

Your spot-the-difference image

To prolong the visibility of the image before it disappears, add the following line just above pygame.quit():

>sleep(3)

By Clicking Run again, the image stays on the screen for a longer period. So you can stick your surprise image by typing the following just below the line pygame.display.update():

>zombie = pygame.image.load('scary_face.png')

>zombie = pygame.transform.scale (zombie, (width, height))

Add a delay, so that the zombie image doesn't appear right away:

> sleep(3)

Thereafter, blit the image to the screen and update so that it reflects to the player:

> screen.blit(zombie, (0,0))
> pygame.display.update()

When you Click on the Run icon, you may start wondering about what will happen; Pygame will basically load your spot-the-difference image, giving you something to be cheerful about. But after three seconds it will be replaced with the scary zombie.

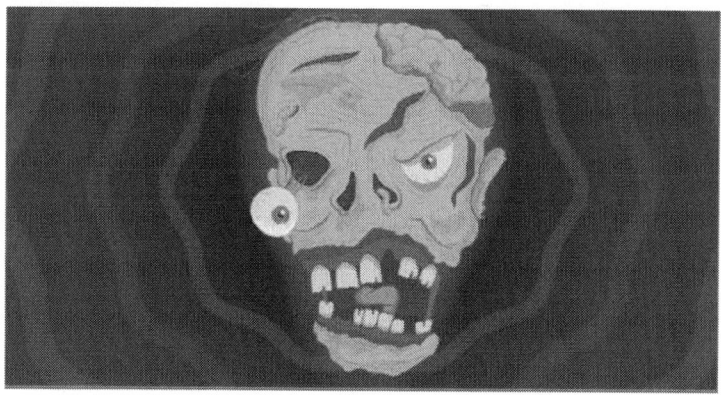

It'll give someone a scary surprise

Having the delay set at three seconds encourages a predictable behaviour that may spoil the fun you intend to have with your friends. You had better change the line sleep(3) above screen.blit(zombie, (0,0)) to:

sleep(randrange(5, 15))

This picks a random number between 5 and 15 while other line of action remains valid. Next, add the following line just above your sleep instruction to load the scream sound file:

scream = pygame.mixer.Sound('scream.wav')

Move below your sleep command and enter the following instruction on a new line to start the sound in a way that it is heard before the ominous image bursts out on the screen:

scream.play()

Finally, tell Pygame to stop playing the sound by typing the following line just above pygame.quit():

scream.stop()

When you hit the Run icon with a wide grin on your lips in anticipation of what you want to do, you will discover that hitting that icon could lead to a scary destination where your scary zombie will appear with a backbreaking shriek which would give your friends the shiver!

If the zombie picture appears before the sound starts playing, you can adjust it by adding a small delay just after your scream.play() instruction and before your screen.blit instruction with this line:

sleep(0.4)

Finally! Your lines of instruction and codes appears like this:

```
import pygame
from pygame.locals import *
from time import sleep
from random import randrange
pygame.init()
width = pygame.display.Info().current_w
height = pygame.display.Info().current_h
screen = pygame.display.set_mode((width, height))
difference = pygame.image.load('spot_the_diff.png')
```

```
difference                                    =
pygame.transform.scale(difference, (width,
height)) screen.blit(difference, (0, 0))
pygame.display.update()
zombie                                        =
pygame.image.load('scary_face.png')
zombie = pygame.transform.scale (zombie,
(width, height)) scream =
pygame.mixer.Sound('scream.wav')
sleep(randrange(5, 15))
scream.play()
screen.blit(zombie, (0,0))
pygame.display.update()
sleep(3)
scream.stop()
pygame.quit()
```

What are you waiting for, invite your friends to play spot-the-difference while the speakers are turned up to the highest volume for sheer excitement.

Chapter 19: Python Project 3- RPG Maze

By now, you are getting the hang of this programming language. Using the Pygame, you can attempt to create an advanced program. Creating more complex than simple programs allows you to enjoy the beauty of this language.

For this advanced program, you can create a fully-functional, text-based maze game. Let us take a classic role-playing exciting game known as interactive fiction which dates back to a period when computers had poor graphics capability. During this period, arcade games plays on the imagination where the simplicity of the characters and missions leaves you amazed.

A fully-functional program is quite complex than the others in this chapter and to introduce this advanced concept to you in a way that you will appreciate and understand, you will commence with a standard version.

1 Open the Chromium Web Browser and go to the following address: rpf.io/rpg-code.

2. The Chromium Web Browser will automatically download the code of the program to your Download folder.

3. Move the cursor on Thonny and click the Load icon. Find the file, rpg-rpg.py, in your Download folder and click on the Load button.

4. To run the downloaded package, Start by clicking the Run icon to familiarise yourself with how a text adventure works. And you can trace the output in the shell area at the bottom of the Thonny window too.

5. For convenience, enlarge the Thonny window by clicking on the maximise button.

The game is quite simple: two rooms and no objects are the available elements. The player hits the ground running in the Hall, busting into the first room of the two rooms.

To enter the Kitchen, type 'go south' followed by the ENTER key.

When you're in the Kitchen, you can issue this command 'go north' to return to the Hall. You can also try typing 'go west' and 'go east', but as there aren't any rooms in those directions the game will show you an error message.

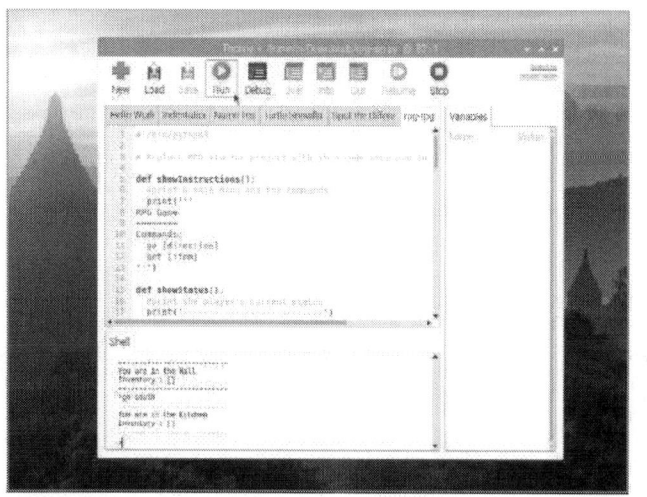

There are only two rooms so far

When you click the Stop icon, and look in the variables area for the rooms variable, you will find the roadmap of the game. This type of variable is essentially a dictionary which provides data about the rooms, their exits, and which room a given exit leads to. If you scroll down to line 29 of the program in the script area, you'll see where this variable is created and how it's laid out.

To make the game more interesting, include another room: perhaps a Dining Room would find a place at the east of the Hall.

Find the rooms variable in the scripts area, and extend it by adding a comma symbol (,) after the } on line 38, then type the following (exact indentation isn't essential in a dictionary):

'Dining Room' : {

'west' : 'Hall'

After you have finished this, You need a new exit in the Hall, as one isn't automatically created for you. Go to the end of line 33, add a comma, then add the following line:

'east' : 'Dining Room'

Click on the Run icon, and see for yourself the magic that just happened in your new room: type 'go east' while in the Hall to enter the Dining Room, and type 'go west' while in the Dining Room to enter the Hall.

Congratulations: you've made a room of your own!

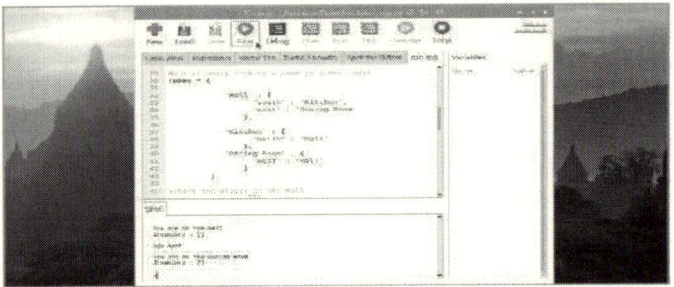

You have added another room

Empty rooms can be quite bored without items. To add an item to a room, the first step is to modify that room's dictionary. Stop the program by clicking the Stop icon. Find the Hall dictionary in the scripts area, then add a comma to the end of the line 'east' : 'Dining Room' before pressing ENTER and typing the following line:

    'item' : 'key'

Click on Run again. This time, the game will tell you that you can see your new item: a key. Type 'get key' and you can pick it up, adding it to the list of items you have created – known as inventory. Your inventory remains with you as you travel from room to room.

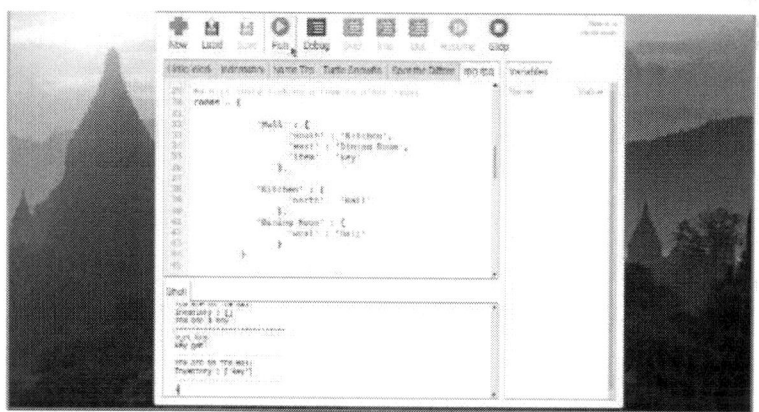

Click the Stop button, and make the game more interesting by adding an obstacle—a monster will do. Include the monster item in the Kitchen dictionary just like you created a value for the key item, add a comma to the end of each line.

'item' : 'monster'

To carry the monster along where it is directly involved in the game, attacking the player or creating problems for the hero; you'll need to add some logic to the game in order to introduce this narrative. Do this by Scrolling to the very bottom of the program in the script area and add the following lines with proper indentation. You could attach the comment too, marked with a hash symbol, which will help you understand the program if you come back to it another day.

player loses if they enter a room with a monster

if 'item' in rooms[currentRoom] and 'monster' in rooms[currentRoom]['item']:

print('A monster has got you... GAME OVER!')

break

Click Run, and try going into the Kitchen room- the monster won't be too impressed when you do!

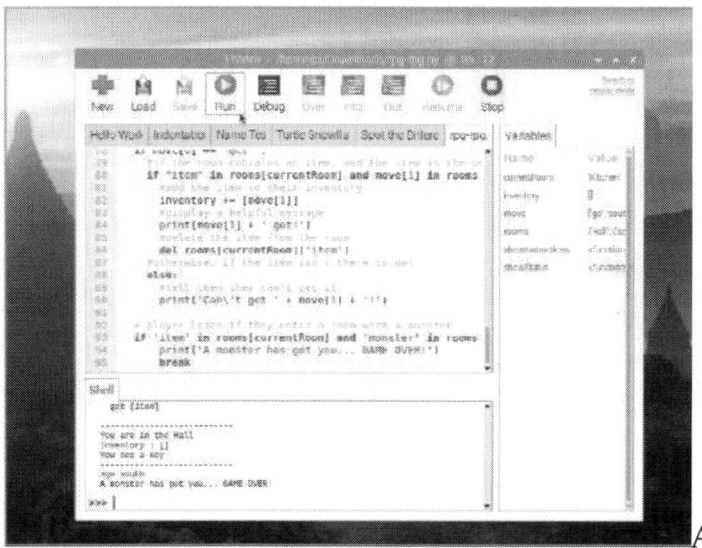

A monster has got you!

To turn this adventure into a proper game, you're going to need more items, another room, and the ability to 'win' by leaving the house with all the items safely in your inventory. Start by adding another room, just as you did for the Dining Room – only this time, it's a Garden. Add an exit from the Dining Room dictionary, remembering to add a comma to the end of the line above:

    'south' : 'Garden'

Then include your new room to the main rooms dictionary, remember to add a comma after the } on the line above as before:

> 'Garden' : {
>
> 'north' : 'Dining Room'

Add a 'potion' object to the Dining Room dictionary while including the necessary comma to the line above:

> 'item' : 'potion'

Finally, scroll to the bottom of the program and add the logic required to check that the player has all the items and, if so, tell them they've won the game:

> # player wins if they get to the garden with a key and a potion
>
> if currentRoom == 'Garden' and 'key' in inventory and 'potion' in inventory:
>
> print('You escaped the house... YOU WIN!')

Click Run, and try to finish the game by picking up the key and the potion before going to the garden. Avoid the Kitchen room because that's where the monster is!

As a last tweak for the game, providing suggestions to the player about the game and how to go about it has nothing to do with breaking rules. You might want to scroll to the top of the program, where the function showInstructions() is defined, and add the following:

> Get to the Garden with a key and a potion.

Avoid the monsters!

Run the game one last time, and you'll see the changes your new lines has created, usually at the very start. Congratulations! you've made an interactive text-based maze game!

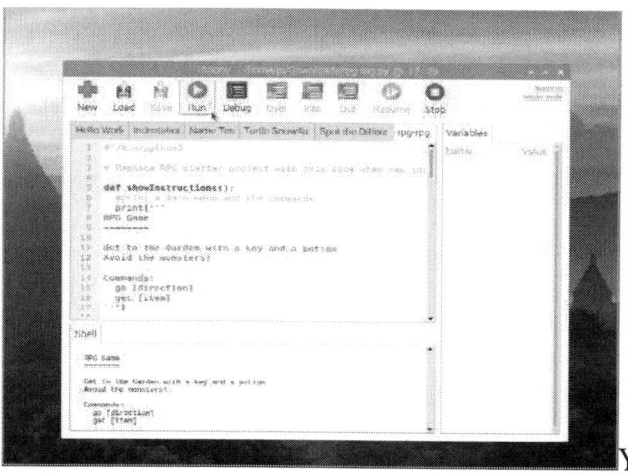
Your text-based game is looking good

CHALLENGE: EXPAND THE GAME

Continue to think about ways to make your adventure more daring. Ask yourself! Can you add more rooms to make the game last longer? Can you include an item to reduce the impact from the claws of the monster? How would you add a weapon to slay the monster? Can you add more rooms that will be above and below the existing rooms, accessed by stairs?

COUNT FROM ZERO

Python is a zero-indexed language which means that it starts counting from 0, not from 1. Whenever you run programs and instructions, Python prints the numbers from 0 through 9 instead of 1 to 10, especially when you are dealing with loops. But you can change this behavior by switching the default range (0, 10) to (1, 11). You can also create wider ranges.

As you are already aware, Indentation is the powerhouse of Python, so you really want to take it serious when you are running your code.

Looking for errors in your code can become daunting, but a process called debugging can lift the burden off your shoulders.

Anyway, a professional tip is that you should not take chances and make a habit of double-checking indentation most especially when you are dealing with nesting loops.

Python also supports infinite loops, which is basically a continuous activity or command. To change your program from a definite loop to an infinite loop, edit line 2 to read: while True:

If you click the Run icon now, your programs will end up in an error feedback because 'i' is not defined and you have also removed the line that created and assigned a value to the variable i. To fix this, simply edit line 3 so it no longer uses the variable:

```
print("Loop running!")
```

Click the Run icon where you will see the 'Loop starting!' message followed by a never-ending string of 'Loop running' messages. As a result of the infinite nature of loop, The 'Loop finished!' message does not print. A takeaway from this section is that whenever Python executes the 'Loop running!' message, it reverts to the beginning of the loop and prints it again.

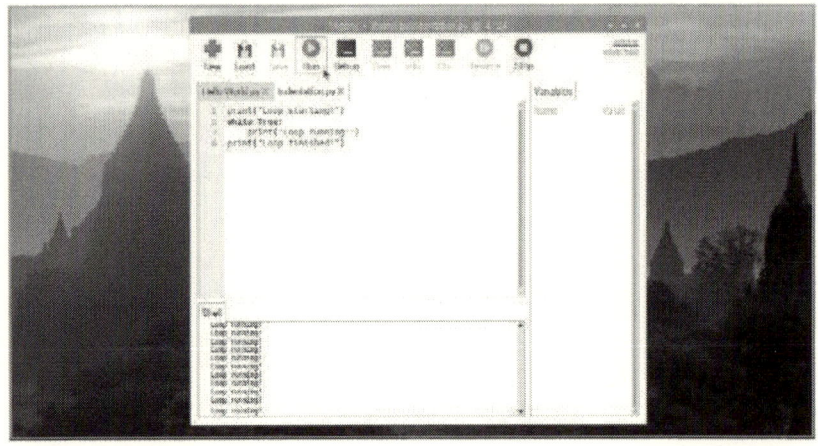

Clicking the Stop icon on the Thonny toolbar drags the program to a halt, a process called interrupting the program. This process is activated when a message appears in the shell area, stopping the instructions from reaching line 4.

CHALLENGE: LOOP THE LOOP

You ought to know how to use loops, including the interplay of definite loops and indefinite loops. And perhaps know how to use loops in very interesting ways. Mastering loops also gives you the ability to add different loops that perform complex functions as a standalone or within a loop. Knowing how and when to use definite and indefinite loops goes a long way in your programming career.

Conditionals and variables

Variables are the bedrock of programming languages, controlling more than just loops. To Start a new program, click on the New icon on the menu bar and type the following into the script area:

userName = input ("What is your name? ")

Click the Run icon, save your program as Name Test, and pay close attention to the shell area: A prompt appears requesting your name. Proceed by typing your name into the shell area, and press ENTER. When you take this action, the variable section close to the right of the Thonny window displays the variable and its value. The variable area remains passive and open regardless of active work in progress, making it convenient to know your program activities.

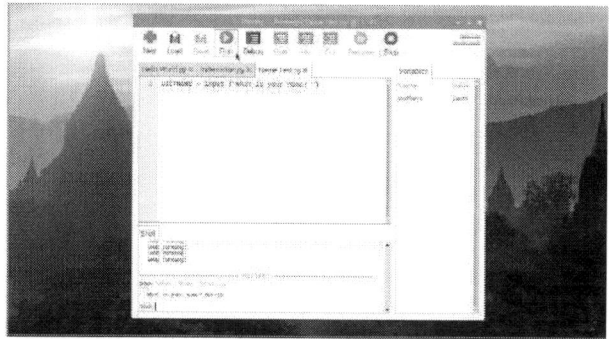

Conditionals allow your program to have a unique narrative. Using conditional statements moves your program in a particular direction. You can use conditionals with a name to create a meaningful program. For example, add a conditional statement by typing the following:

```
if userName == "Clark Kent":

    print("You are Superman!") else:

    print("You are not Superman!")
```

The rules of indentation still applies here with conditionals, so you might want to hit the BACKSPACE key often to reduce spaces yourself in order to prevent error feedback.

Click the Run icon and enter your name into the shell area. Unless your name happens to be Clark Kent, you'll see the message 'You are not Superman!'. When you click Run again while entering the name 'Clark Kent', endeavor to write it exactly like the program, with an upper case C and upper case K. After doing this, the program recognizes that you are, in fact, Superman.

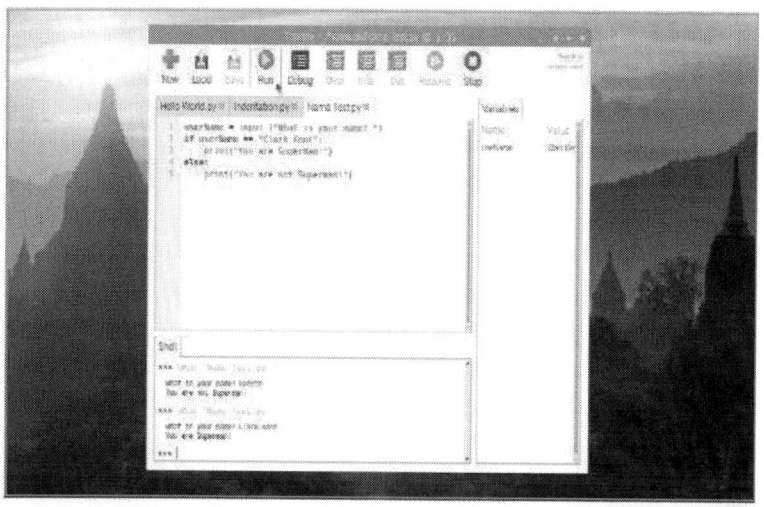

The == symbols instructs Python to do a direct comparison, looking to see that the variable userName matches the text – known as a string – in your program. If you're working with numbers, you can make comparisons with certain symbols known as comparison operators.

> indicates that a number is greater than another number,

< indicates that a number is less than another number.

=> indicates that a number is equal to or greater than another number.

=< indicates a number is equal to or less than another number.

!= indicates that a number is not equal to another number; the exact opposite of ==.

USING = AND ==

Knowing Python's variable is not as important as using them when it counts. = means 'make this variable equal to this value', while == means 'check to see if the variable is equal to this value'. Using both variables lead to a dead end because they simply do not go together.

Comparison operators can also be used in loops. Delete line2 through 5, then type the following in their place:

while userName != "Clark Kent":

print("You are not Superman - try again!")

userName = input ("What is your name? ")
print("You are Superman!")

Click the Run icon again. This time, rather than quitting, the program will keep asking for your name until it confirms that you are Superman– sort of like a very simple password. To get out of the loop, either type 'Clark Kent' or click the Stop icon on the Thonny toolbar.

Congratulations: you now know how to use conditionals and comparison operators!

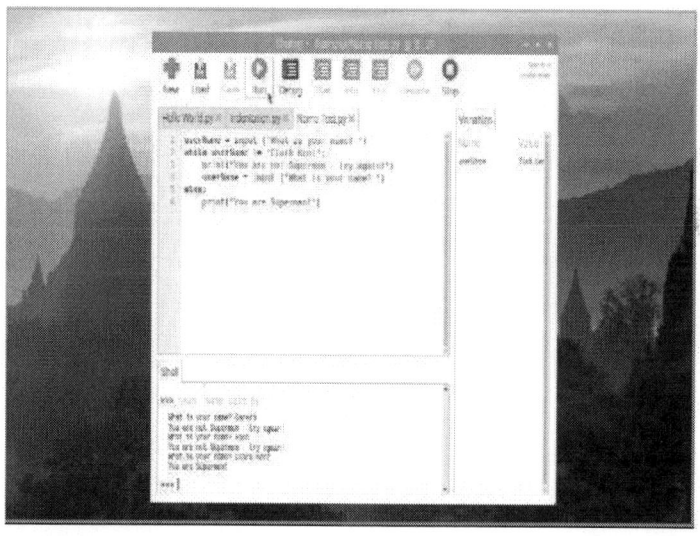

CHALLENGE: ADD MORE QUESTIONS

Can you change the program to ask more than one question while storing the answers in multiple variables?

Can you create a program with a bunch of conditionals and comparison operators to print a random number typed in by the end user which is higher or lower than 5

Chapter 20: Physical Computing with Raspberry Pi 4

Like the name, physical computing is when you write some programs that work with hardware to give a physical action, like move, jump, and so on. Best example is your washing machine. You switch it on and set the temperature or the spinning rate to your desired level. The washing machine starts working and performs a physical action with the press of buttons. That is Physical Computing at work.

Learning about physical computing can get a lot easier with the help of Raspberry – a cool tool to learn physical computation better. Its key component is the general-purpose input/output (GPIO) header.

Introduction to GPIO Header

The GPIO header is located at the top edge of the Pi circuit board that looks like 2 rows of iron pin. It is the way to connect the light-emitting diodes (LEDs) and switches which are the hardware to the Pi for the programs you have written in order to give you a physical computing output.

The name, even though sounds confusing but defines its features well. You can use the pins for input and output, as they serve more than one purpose. When pins are in the open such as this, they are called Header which brings us back to the initial name: General-purpose input/output header

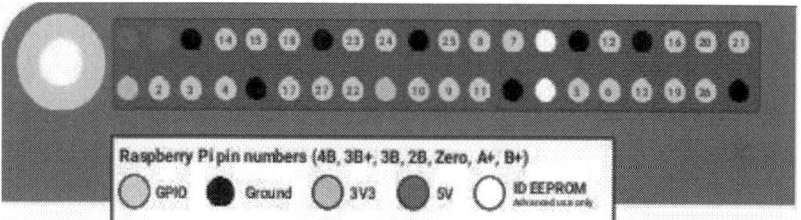

There are 40 male pins of which the Raspberry Pi GPIO header consists of some of which are accessible to use for physical computation while some produces power and others are reserved for add-on hardware communication such as the Sense HAT.

Pin types are categorized into several ways with each having a defined function:

3V3	3.3 volts power	A permanently-on source of 3.3 V power, the same voltage the Raspberry Pi runs at internally
5V	5 volts power	A permanently-on source of 5 V power, the same voltage as the Raspberry Pi takes in at the micro USB power connector
Ground (GND)	0 volts ground	A ground connection, used to complete a circuit connected to power source
GPIO XX	General-purpose input/output pin number XX	The GPIO pins available for your programs, identified by a number from 2 to 27
ID EEPROM	Reserved special-purpose pins	Pins reserved for use with Hardware Attached on Top (HAT) and other accessories

WARNING!

You have to be careful with dealing with Raspberry Pi's GPIO header.

Do not bend the pins in the connecting and disconnecting process of the hardware. Two pins should never be connected one at a time or except you are instructed to do so in a project. Connecting two pins at a time is called short circuit and it can destroy the PI permanently.

Electronic Components

What you need to commence your physical computing consist of the GPIO header and other electrical features that will be controlled from the GPIO header. There are lots of components but GPIO projects are mostly done with the use of these common parts.

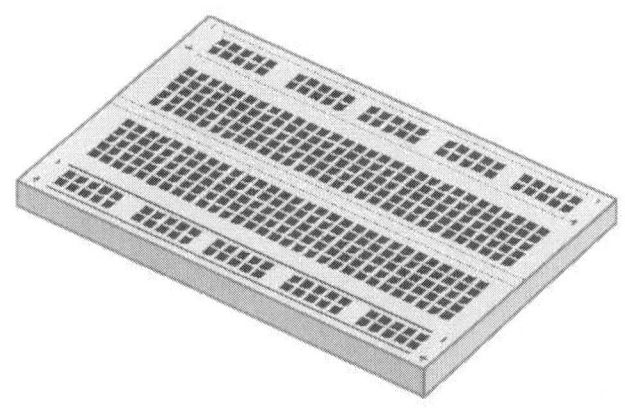

Breadboard: This make your physical computing way easier. You will need not to go through connecting several components wires with Breadboard; it lets you do that easily with the metal tracks below its upper surface. Breadboards also have power distributions that let you create your circuit easily.

Even though it is not a must to have, but you will save yourself some stress using Breadboard. It can also be called Solderless.

Jumper Wires: This connects your electrical components with the Raspberry Pi. There are three versions of Jumper wires; M2F (male-to-female), it is needed to connect your solderless to the GPIO pins; F2F (female-to-female), it makes it possible to connect component individually when you are not using a solderless; M2M (male-to-male).

This is a tool for connecting across the solderless. You will need these three types of Jumper wire depending on your project. M2M and M2F can be avoided when you are using a Solderless.

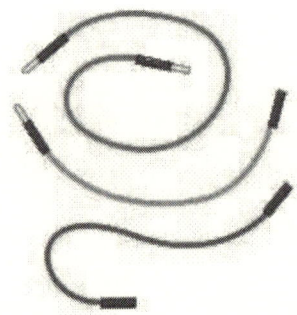

Push Button Switch: It can also be called a momentary switch. This is the kind of switch that is used in the controller of game consoles. It usually comes with 2 or 4 stands, whichever one will do just fine with the Raspberry's Pi. The push button serves as an input device that lets you command your program to perform a certain action.

Other types of switch is Latching switch, where you will have to hold down the push button before it becomes active. Latching switch can be activated at one toggle and can be deactivated when toggled again.

Light-emitting diode (LED): Unlike the Push-button, LED serves as an output device and can directly be controlled from your program. It comes up when on, and can be found all around your building, from the small one to the big ones.

They come in various shapes, sizes and colors. However, not all LED are compatible to use with Raspberry PI. Some are designed for 12 V or 5 V power supplies, please avoid them.

Resistors: This is the component that is in charge of controlling the current flow and is in different values which can be measured in ohms (Ω).

The resistance provides resistors based on the number of ohms. In Raspberry Pi physical computing projects, the resistor is usually used to safeguard the LEDs from attracting excess electric current and destroy one another. You will need a resistor of 330 ohms to create more flexibility.

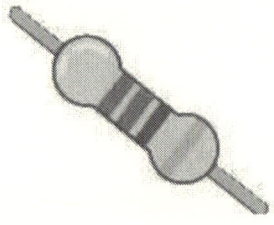

Piezoelectric buzzer: also called a sounder is an output device but not like an LED that produces light. Buzzer is an output device that produces a buzzing noise. Piezoelectric buzzer contains two metal plates that vibrate opposing each other when activated. Buzzer has two types which are active and passive. An active buzzer is the perfect choice on your physical computing.

Motor is another recognized component that requires a special control board to get tit connected to the Pi. Infrared sensors are a device that detects the temperature, humidity sensors and movement. Also the LDRs which mean light-dependent resistors are an input device that works like reverse LED.

Sellers all over the world provide components for physical computing with the Raspberry Pi, either as individual parts or in kits which provide everything you need to get started. Some of the most popular retailers are:
Retailers' worldwide stock electrical components for physical computing along with the Raspberry Pi, they sell in bit or in kit that gets you started. These are some of the notable sellers around the world:

- **RS Components – uk.rs-online.com**
- **CPC – cpc.farnell.com**
- **ModMyPi – modmypi.com**
- **Pi Hut – thepihut.com**
- **PiSupply – uk.pi-supply.com**
- **Adafruit – adafruit.com**
- **Pimoroni – pimoroni.com**

To complete the projects in this chapter, you should have at least:

- 3 × LEDs: green, yellow, and red or amber
- 2 × push-button switches
- 1 × active buzzer
- Male-to-female (M2F) and female-to-female (F2F) jumper wires
- Optionally, a breadboard and male-to-male (M2M) jumper wires

Reading Resistor Color Codes

There is a spectrum of values for resistor starting from zero-resistance version that is made up of just small pieces of wire to the high-resistance versions of the size of which can be compared to a human leg.

However, you can only see the value written on only a few of these resistors which are usually in stripe color on the resistor

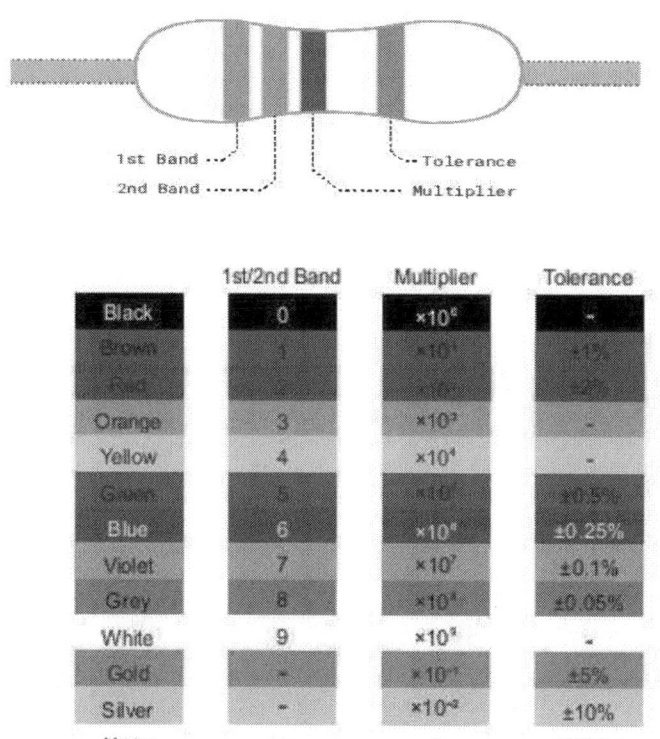

You can read the value of a resistor by positioning the bands to the left and lone band to the right. Now the first thing to look out for in the first band is the color which can be found in the 1st/2nd Band' of the table to acquire the 1st and 2nd figure.

There are two orange bands in this example with both having the same value '3' and makes a total of '33'.

Your band may have more than 3 bands; you will have to write down what the value of the third band is (for five/six-band resistors, see rpf.io/5-6band).

Now go to the last group of bands and check for the color of either the third or fourth band, it can be found in the 'Multiplier' section.

It informs you about the number you will multiply the present number by to get the right value of your resistor.

There is a scientific notation 'x10^1' that stands as a brown band in this example which translates to 'include a 0 to the last number'. For blue, it is x10^6 which means to add six 0s to end of the number.

The orange band is 33 with the addition of the 0 from the brown band, it will make it 330: The resistor's value that is measured in ohms.

On the right is the final banding that serves as a tolerant for the resistor. It is likely to be near its value this way: Since cheaper resistors are bound to have a silver band, when trying to figure out its exact value, it may go 10% higher or lower than the actual value.

There is no band which indicates that it can go 20% higher or lower, this is because resistors that are the most expensive comes with grey bands which means that it is just in between 0.05% of actual rating. You really need no precision if you are on hobbyist projects.

Values of resistors that are over 1000 ohms are measured in kiloohms (kΩ) and if it is over 1 million ohms they are called megohms (MΩ). You have 2200 Ω resistor indicated as 2.2 kΩ while 2200000 Ω would be indicated as 2.2 MΩ.

Chapter 21: Your first Physical Computing Program: Hello, LED!

Creating the LED light is the beginning of the journey to learning physical computing just as writing 'hello world' to the screen is the traditional start to learning programming. On this project, an LED with a 330 ohm resistor will be needed or any rating close to 330 ohm with a F2F (female-to-female) jumper wires.

RESISTANCE IS VITAL

The resistor plays an important role in the circuit because it serves as a protection for the LED and the Raspberry Pi by giving a limit to the electrical current flow that the LED draws. Without the resistor, the electrical current can become excessive for the LED which could lead to burning itself or even the PI.

When it is utilized this way, it serves as the current-limiting resistor. The precise value of resistor you will use will be determined by the LED in use. However, the resistor whose value is 330 ohm works for most LEDs.

The effects of the resistors value work like this on the LED: When a resistor value is higher, the LED becomes dimmer and when the value is lower, the LED is brighter. Do not connect the Pi and the LED together without the interference of the current-limiting resistor only if the LED comes with a built-in resistor of the required value.

1. Begin your work by confirming if your LED is functioning.

2. Position the Raspberry Pi in a way that will separate the GPIO header into 2 vertical stripes off to the right.

3. Make a connection of Raspberry Pi with first 3.3 V pin.

4. With the use of a F2F jumper wire.

5. Join the other end to the log leg to either the anode or positive of your LED using yet another F2F jumper wire.

6. Pick the last F2F jumper wire and join the short leg with either the cathode or negative of the LED to the first ground pin.

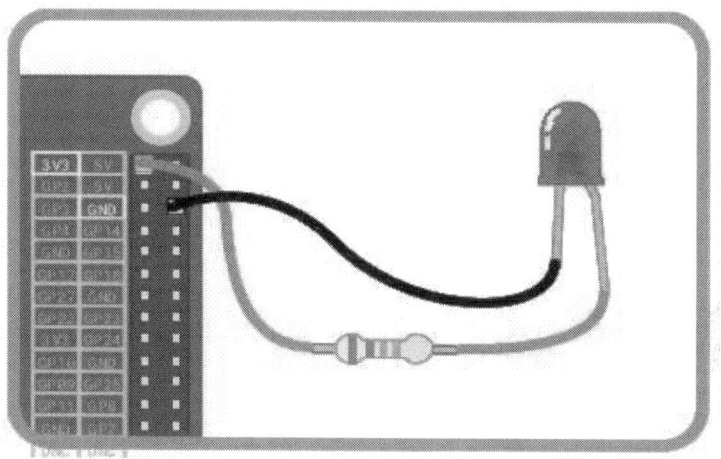

7. Connect your LEDs to these pins and do not forget the resistor.

8. In as much as you have your Raspberry Pi on, the LED light will be up.

9. And if in case it does not, cross check your circuits to confirm whether you are doing it exactly as you are being taught.

10. Check the connections and ensure that the resistor value is not too high for your LED and the Raspberry Pi.

After you have confirmed that your LED is working, now it is time to do the programming.

1. Disconnect the 3.3 V pin from the jumper wire and connect a jumper wire to the GPIO 25 pin. This will make the LED go off, when it happens, do not fret, it is okay.

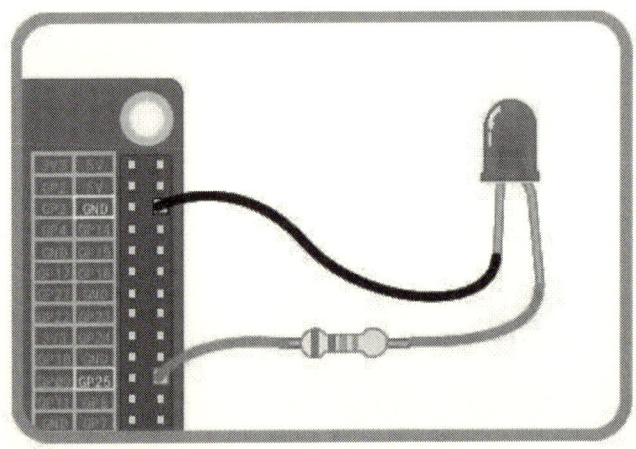

11. After you have confirmed that your LED is working, now it is time to do the programming. Disconnect the 3.3 V pin from the jumper wire and connect a jumper wire to the GPIO 25 pin. This will make the LED go off, when it happens, do not fret, it is okay.

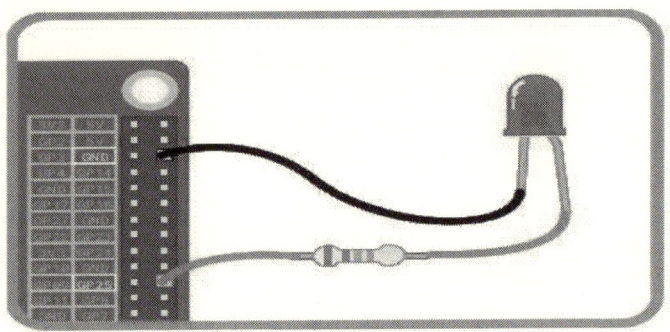

Now it is time to create a Python or Scratch to control the power switch of the LED.

CODING KNOWLEDGE

You have to be able to use the Thonny Python IDE and the Scratch 2 comfortably to be able to continue this project.

LED Control in Scratch

You can load the Scratch 2 in the Raspberry menu.

Press 'More Blocks' in the blocks column and click the 'Add an Extension' key. Now press the 'Pi GPIO' then press OKAY.

This will load all the needed blocks to you and the control on Pi's GPIO header on Scratch 2. The new blocks will appear in the blocks section when they are needed. You can also find them at the More Blocks category.

The *Pi.GPIO extension to Scratch 2*

1. Drag the `when clicked` events block the scripts section.

2. Place the `set gpio to output` under it. It will require you to choose the amount of pin in use:

3. Press the little arrow icon to expand the drop-down selection and press 25 to inform Scratch that you are in control of the GPIO 25 pin.

4. Press the green flag to start your program. Your LED will light up which means that your first physical computing is successfully programmed.

5. Press the red octagon key to end your program. Is the LED is still on?

Yes, the reason is that your program only informed the Pi to switch on the LED. That is the meaning of the `set gpio 25 to output high` block.

6. Switch it off again and press the down arrow key located at the end block and select from the list the 'Output low'.

7. Press the green flag again, this time around; the LED will be turned off as a result of your program.

8. To spice things up, include a `forever` block and some `wait 1 secs` blocks to invent ON and OFF flash on the LED every second.

Keep watching your LED while you press the green flag button. The LED will come up for a second and go off in another second and will keep on repeating this action until you decide to press the red octagon button to put an end to it.

This is what happens when the LED is going on and off and the red octagon button is clicked.

CHALLENGE: CAN YOU ALTER IT?

How to change the program to command the LED to stay on or goes off for a longer period of time? The smallest delay that can be used while the LED is going on and off:

LED Control in Python

Thonny can be loaded from the programming area of the Raspberry menu.

Press the NEW button to get a new project underway and click 'Save', it will be saved as Hello LED. A library known as GPIO zero is needed to be able to get access to the GPIO pin from Python.

Only the part of the library is required to work with LEDs on this project. Import the area of this library by inputting the below into the Python shell section:

from gpiozero import LED

Next, you have to let GPIO Zero understand which GPIO pin is connected to the LED. Write the below code:

led = LED(25)

Both lines let Python control LEDs that are connected to the Pi's GPIO pin and inform it which (pin) s. If the LEDs in your circuit are more than two, you will have to write the below code to control it.

led.on()

To turn of the LED again, write:

led.off()

Well Done! You now have the ability to control the Raspberry Pi's GPIO pin that is in Python. Attempt to write those codes again. When the LED is off the led.off() will not be effective, the same thing happens when the LED is on and your write led.on().

To make a real code, write the below code into the script section:

from gpiozero import LED from time import sleep

led = LED(25)

while True:

    led.on()

    sleep(1)

    led.off()

    sleep(1)

This code will import the LED from the GPIOZero library and also the Sleep function. After this, it will build an infinite loop to switch the LED on for a sec and off for another sec continuously. Press the Run key to watch the action: The LED will start flashing. And for the Scratch program, record the performance when you press the Stop button when the LED is switched on and when it is off.

CHALLENGE: LONGER LIGHT-UP

How to alter the program for the LED to stay ON or OFF for a longer period of time? The smallest delay that can be used while the LED is going on and off.

Using a Breadboard

The project we are about to dive into in this chapter will be much easier if you make use of a breadboard to keep the components together to connect the electric features.

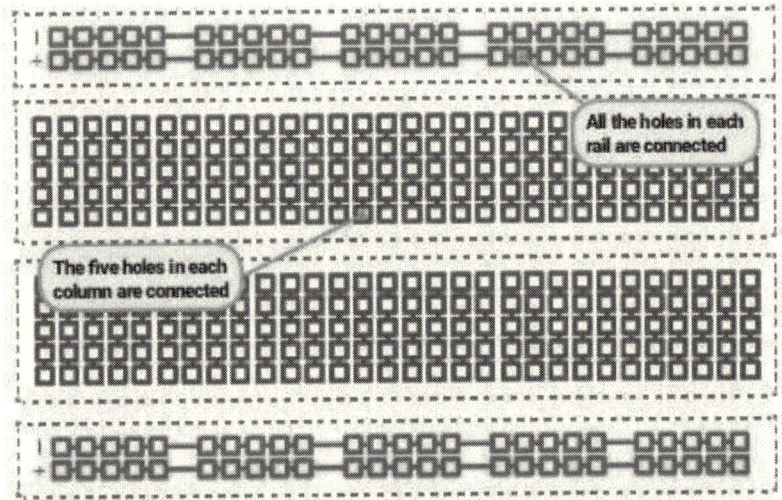

There are holes that cover the breadboards to match with the components, apart from 2.54 mm. Metals strips are found under these holes and serves as the jumper wires that have been in use till now. They operate in rows all across the breadboard that always has a gap across its middle to separate into two.

Majority of breadboards have letters over the top and numbers written below the sides.

This gives you the ability to locate the specific hole: A1, the left corner. B1: the hole to the immediate right. B2: a hole down from there. The hidden metal connects the A1 to B1 but the number 1 hole is always connected to the second hole except you add a jumper wire.

On bigger breadboards, there are strips of holes at the down sides that are in color red, blue or black stripes. They are known as the power rails which makes the wiring process a lot easier.

Connect a wire right from the Pi's ground pin to one of the power rails that are usually in blue, red, black or minus sign (-) to give a ground for many features of the breadboard and same can be done if 3.3 V or 5 V power is required in your circuit.

It is quite easy to add electronic features to a breadboard: Put their leads in line (the sticky-out metal area) with the holes and carefully until it is put in place.

To connect, you have to make more than what the breadboard has provided. M2M can be used; to connect from the breadboards to the Pi, make use of the M2F jumper wires.

Do not memorize more than a jumper wire or component lead into a hole on the breadboard. Since holes are in rows apart from the separation down the middle, the component lead within A1 is connected electrically to whatever you include to B1, C1, D1, and E1.

Chapter 22: Reading a Button

When you see 'input/output' portion of 'GPIO', it means that pins can be used as inputs as well. Things you will need for this project are breadboard, M2M, M2F with a push-button switch. F2F can be used in case you do not have a breadboard available; however, you will find it more difficult to press without breaking the circuit.

Begin with the adding of a push-key to the breadboard. Your push-key has two legs? Ensure that they are in different rows on the breadboard. If your push-key has four legs, change its position to make the sides at which the legs pops out from are in line with the holes on the breadboards and the smooth legless sides are positioned at the top of the bottom. Make a connection of the ground rail to the ground pin of the Raspberry Pi. With the M2M jumper wire.

Now make a connection of a leg on of your push-key with the ground rail using an M2M jumper wire.

And lastly, join the second leg of your push-key, in case you are using a four legged switch to your GPIO 2 pin of the Pi with a M2F jumper wire.

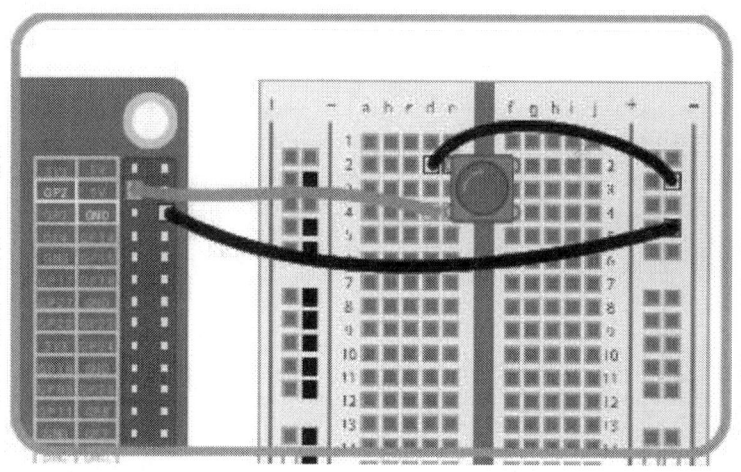

Reading a Button in Scratch

Drag the when clicked events block to the scripts section. Place the set gpio to output block under it. Choose the no 2 from the drop-down to suit the GPIO pin in use for the push-key.

1. Press on the down arrow key located at the end of the block.
2. Then select 'input' from the list to set the pin as input.

Nothing will take effect if you click the green flag and that is a result of what you told the Scratch to do which is to utilize the pin as input and not what you do with it.

3. Move a `forever` block to the end of the sequence and drag an `if then else` block into it. Look for the 'gpio is high? Block and move it into the white space found at the 'if then' area of the block.

4. Make use of the drop down to choose the no 2 to inform which GPIO pin you want to check. Lastly, move a `say hello! for 2 secs` block into the `else` area on the block and alter it to 'Button Pushed!'. Ignore the 'if then' portion on the block for the time being. There are lots of things to get done; however, we can start with the test:

5. Press the green flag and press the key on your breadboard. You will know when the key is pushed and that means an input from the GPIO pin has been read successfully. The `gpio 2 is high? then` part may be empty. The running code when the key has been pressed. It is located in the 'else' part of the block.

6. Does pressing the button makes it go up? Yes, that is quite confusing, the Pi's GPIO are on or goes up when configured as input while pushing the button takes them down.

7. Crosscheck your circuit: confirm if the key has been connected to the GPIO 2 pin that produces the anode area of the circuit with the ground pin.

8. When you push the button, the GPIO pin's voltage win go low along with the ground pin and the Scratch program will cease the code that is running in your `if gpio 2 is high?` then stop and run the code found in the `else` area of the block.

If that sounds confusing, just keep this in mind: a key on a Raspberry Pi GPIO pin is pressed when the pin moves down and not with it goes up.

For expansion of your program, including the LED and resistor back in the circuit: Do not forget to connect the GPIO 25 pin to the resistor and the longer leg of the LED and the shorter leg of the LED to the breadboard's ground rail.

9. To delete it, move the `say Button pushed! for 2 secs` block away from the scripts part to the block palette. And put `set gpio 25 to output high` block as the replacement without forgetting that you will change the GPIO number by making use of the drop down menu.

Include a `set gpio 25 to output low` block and don't forget to alter the value to the empty the `if gpio 2 is high? then` portion on the block.

CHALLENGE: MAKE IT STAY LIT

This is how to alter the program to command the LED to stay on for a couple of seconds even when the button has not been pressed. If you want the LED to stay on when you don't press the button and goes off when you do, how would you go about it?

Reading A Button In Python

Press the New key in Thonny to begin a new project, and press on the Save key. Save it as Key Input. There is huge similarity in the use of a GPIO as an input for a button and a pin as an output for LED. The difference is that you will have to import a portion of the GPIO zero library. Write the below script section:

from gpiozero import Button = Button(2)

To have the code run when the button is pressed, GPIO Zero provides the wait_for_press function. Type the following:

button.wait_for_press()

print("You pushed me!")

Tap the Run key and then click the push-button. Your input will be printed to the shell of the Python that can be found at the down part of the Thonny window:

An input has been read from the GPIO pin then click the GPIO pin. In case you want to retry the program, re-click the Run key which will stop immediately it is done with the printing of the message to the shell because the program contains no loop.

For expansion of your program, including the LED and resistor back in the circuit: Do not forget to connect the GPIO 25 pin to the resistor and the longer leg of the LED and the shorter leg of the LED to the breadboard's ground rail.

If you want to control the LED and read a button, importing the Button and LED function from GPIO zero library is important.

Also, the sleep function will be needed. You can scroll back to the top of the program and write the below as the new 1st two lines:

from gpiozero import LED from time import sleep

Below the line button = Button(2), write:

led = LED(25)

Clear the line print("You pushed me!") and instead input:

led.on() sleep(3) led.off()

Your program should look like this when done: from gpiozero import LED

from time import sleep
from gpiozero import Button
button = Button(2)
led = LED(25) button.wait_for_press() led.on()
sleep(3)
led.off()

Press the Run key and tap the push-button: the LED light will ON for three seconds, then go off after. You can now control an LED using the key from Python.

CHALLENGE: ADD A LOOP

How to add a loop to repeat the program? What are the things that must be altered to let the LED stays on when you do not click on it and OFF when you do?

Chapter 23: Make Some Noise: Controlling a Buzzer

LEDs serve as unique output device but too much of LED cannot be used if you are aiming for another direction. Here is the solution: Buzzer, it produces quite audible noise in the room.

Things you will need for this project include M2F, breadboard and a functioning buzzer. You can use F2F jumper wires to connect your buzzer in case you do not have a breadboard. You can use the same treatment of the LED for an active buzzer when it comes to programming or circuitry.

You can use the circuit you use for LED for the buzzer. But use the active buzzer in place of the LED and then leave out the resistor, because the buzzer requires more current to function.

A leg of the buzzer should be connected to the GPIO 15 and the second leg to the ground pin (as in GND in the diagram) with the use of the breadboard and M2F jumper wires.

Your buzzer may be a three legged one, just ensure that you mark the leg with a minus sign – and connect it to the ground pin and also mark it with 'SIGNAL' or S connecting it to the GPIO 15, and the left leg should be connected to the 3.3 V pin (labeled 3V3.)

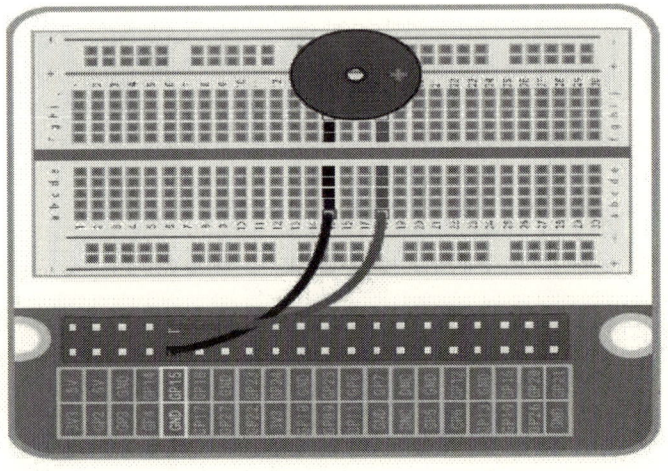

Figure 6-5: Connecting a buzzer to the GPIO pins

Controlling A Buzzer In Scratch

The program process should go as the LED flash went or you can load it if it was saved before the creation of the button project. Make use of the drop-down option that can be found in the set gpio to output high blocks to choose number 15, thus, Scratch is in control of the right GPIO pin. Press the green flag for your buzzer to start buzzing: If you hear the buzzer clicking just once in a second, then that is a passive buzzer and not an active one.

An active buzzer will generate a fast changing signal for the metal plates to vibrate itself which is oscillating.

A passive buzzer on the other hand will require an oscillating signal. The plates make movement once when it is switched on with Scratch that makes the sound 'click' till the program turns off or on the switch.

Push the red octagon button to put an end to the buzz; however, ensure that it is done when it is not ringing or else, it will continue buzzing until the program reruns.

CHALLENGE: CHANGE THE BUZZ

How to alter the program for the buzzer to buzz for a shorter period of time? How to create a circuit that controls the buzzer with a button?

Controlling a buzzer in Python

The control of an active buzzer with the GPIO zero library is similar to the control of a LED. There is ON and OFF states. Different function will be required even though there is a buzzer. Begin a new project on Thonny, save Buzzer and write the below code:

from gpiozero import Buzzer from time import sleep

As it is with LEDs, GPIO Zero has to understand which of the pins your buzzer is connected to for the control. Write the following:

> *buzzer = Buzzer(15)*

It is now the same as the one for LED; the only difference (apart from a different GPIO pin number) is that it is the buzzer being used and not a led.

Input the below:

while True:
> *buzzer.on()*
> *sleep(1)*
> *buzzer.off()*
> *sleep(1)*

Press the green flag for your buzzer to start buzzing: If the buzzer is heard clicking just once in a second then that is a passive buzzer and not an active one. An active buzzer will generate a fast changing signal for the metal plates to vibrate itself which is oscillating. A passive buzzer on the other hand will require an oscillating signal.

Press the Stop key to close the program but ensure that the buzzer is not buzzing at that moment or else it will keep on the buzz until you decide to make a rerun of the program.

CHALLENGE: A BETTER BUZZ

How to alter the program for the buzzer to buzz for a shorter period of time? How to create a circuit that controls the buzzer with a button?

Chapter 24: Scratch project: Traffic Lights

You can now use LEDs, buzzers and buttons as output and input devices which set you ready to create a real physical computing. The traffic light is programmed with a button you can push to cross the road.

Things you will need for this project are three 330 ohms resistors; a yellow, red, and green LED; a breadboard, a push button-switch, and M2M, M2F jumper wires.

Commence from the circuit, making a connection of the GPIO 15 pin to the buzzer, LED in red to GPIO 25 pin, the

LED in yellow to GPIO 8, the LED in green to GPIO 7 and the switch to GPIO 2.

Do not forget to join the 330 ohms resistor within the GPIO pins to the LED with the longer legs, and the 2nd legs to be connected to the components of the ground nail. Lastly, On the Raspberry Pi, join the ground rail to the pin (GND) to complete the circuit.

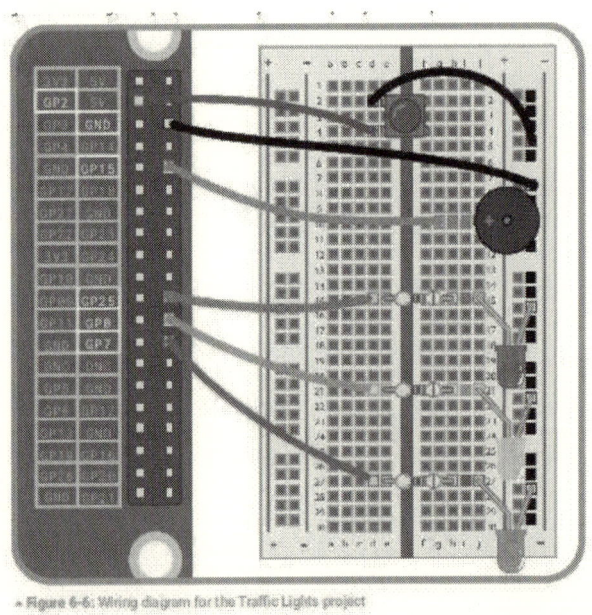

Figure 6-6: Wiring diagram for the Traffic Lights project

Begin a new scratch 2 project and move the when clicked events block to the scripts section.

Now inform the Scratch that GPIO 2 pin that is joined with the push-button switch in the circuit is an input device and not output.

Move the 'set gpio to output high' block from the 'More Blocks' section of the blocks palette below the when clicked block. Press the down arrow key beside 'o' and choose no 2 from the drop down list and press the arrow beside 'output high' and choose 'input'.

You will have to create the traffic light sequence next. Move the 'forever' block to the current program and fill it with blocks in order to switch on the traffic light LEDs and off in a specific way. Do not forget the GPIO pins and their respective components. When the pin 25 is being used, the red LED is in use. Yellow LED for pin 8, and green LED for pin 7.

Tap the green flag and look at the LEDs: the red light will come up first and then red and yellow light will come together at a time and then green and then yellow, lastly the red light will end the sequence again. This style is similar to the UK traffic lights; however, you can customize it to fit in for any other countries.

To duplicate a pedestrian crossing, your program must look out for the right button to press.

Tap the red octagon to put an end to the program when it is running. Move the 'if then else' block to the script and connect it to be positioned under the forever block with the traffic sequence in the 'if then' are, Ignore the 'if then' portion on the block for the time being.

Pedestrian crossing lights change the red light immediately you push the button, it waits for the line coming next in the sequence. To simulate that to your program, move the 2nd 'when clicked' block to the script section and then the 'forever' block should follow.

Move the 'if then' block underneath your 'forever' block and input the 'not' operator into the blank and then followed with 'gpio 2 is high?' block without forgetting to utilize the drop-down section to alter the GPIO pin number. Lastly, build a PUSHED variable and put a 'set pushed to 1' block into the 'if then' block.

The block stack job is to look out for the pushed button and adjust the variable **'pushed'** to 1.

Adjustment of a variable with this method allows you to save the pushed button even when you are not ready to work on it.

Return to the main block stack and look for 'if then' block. Move the = Operator block into the 'if then' block in blank diamond-shaped space and move the 'pushed' reporter block to the first square-shaped blank. Input '0' into the 2nd blank.

Tap the green flag, look as the traffic lights pass through their paths. Push the push-button switch: No traces will be seen at first but when the sequence has reached its destination, then the lights will be off and stay off with the help of the 'pushed' variable.

The remaining work left is making the button work for other stuff than switching off the light. Look for the 'else' block and move the `set gpio 25 to output high` block in it without forgetting to alter the default setting for the GPIO pin number to suit the red LED's pin. Under that in the 'else' block, make a pattern for your buzzer: move the 'repeat 10' block, then input `set gpio 15 to output high`, 'wait 0.2 secs', `set gpio 25 to output`, and 'wait 0.2 secs' block and change the GPIO pin value to the buzzer's pin yet again.

Lastly, under the bottom part of your 'repeat 10' block yet in the 'else' block, include a `set pushed to o` block and `a set gpio 25 to output low` block the final block to reset the variable that saved the key press to limit the repetition of the buzzer.

Tap the green flag and press the switch on the breadboard. The red light will come up and the buzzer will sound to inform the pedestrians that the cross is safe. The buzzer will stop after a few seconds and the traffic will continue yet again until the button is pressed.

Hurray! Your traffic light is set to go.

CHALLENGE: CAN YOU IMPROVE IT?

How do you alter the program to let the pedestrian cross for a longer time? Can you reprogram your traffic light to fit in to other countries? How can you dim the LED light?

Chapter 25: Python project: Quick Reaction Game

LEDs and buttons can now be used as input and output devices, you can now be set to create a real physical computing. Two-player quick-reaction game created to discover whose reaction is the fastest. Things you will need for this project are LED, breadboard, a 330 ohm resistor, 2 push-button switches, M2Fs and M2M jumper wires.

Firstly, you will build a circuit: make a connection of both the switch at the left of your board and the GPIO 14 pin (labeled GP14, Fig 6-7). The 2nd switch at the breadboard's right to GPIO 15 pin (labeled GP15), and the longer leg of the LED should be connected to the 330 ohm resistor and join the GPIO 4 pin (labeled GP4) of your Raspberry Pi and the 2nd leg on every component on the ground rail.

Lastly, make a connection of the ground rail and Raspberry Pi's ground pin (labeled GND).

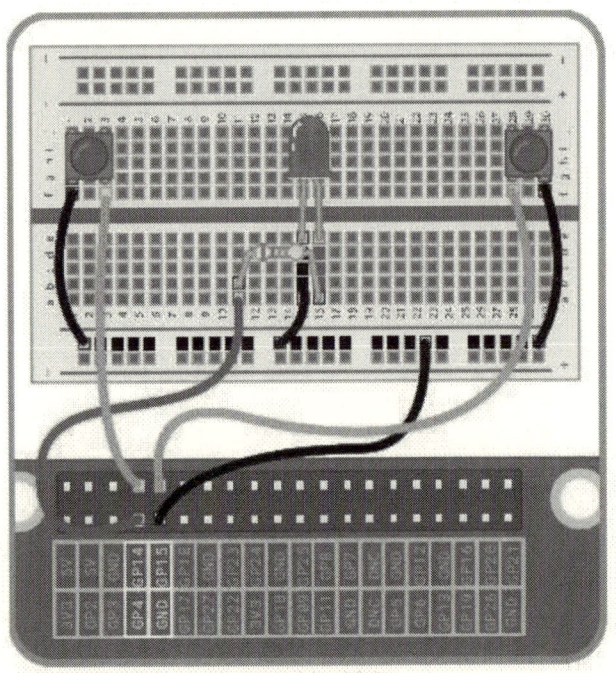

Figure 6-7: Wiring diagram for the Quick Reaction Game

On Thonny, launch a new project which is to be saved as Reaction Game. You will need the button and LED functions from the GPIOZero library with the sleep function too. They can be saved and import together using a comma sign (,) to divide them. Write the below in the script section:

from gpiozero import LED, Button from time import sleep

As usual, inform the GPIO Zero which of the pins are the two buttons and the LED are connected to. Write the below:

led = LED(4) right_button = Button(15) left_button = Button(14)

Now include instructions to switch the LED on and off, to confirm if it is working perfectly:

led.on() sleep(5) led.off()

Press the Run key, this will make the LED come up for 5 secs and go off then the program will exit. The light going off at a fixed time can be predictable, include the following line from the time import sleep:

from random import uniform

The random library allows you to shuffle and garner random numbers(with a uniform distribution- rpf.io/uniform). Search for the sleep(5) and alter it to the below:

sleep(uniform(5, 10))

Tap on the Run key again: This will make the LED remain lit at random seconds around 5 – 10. Observe and read the time it takes for the LED to come off and press the RUN KEY few times more: there will be different time interval for every run which makes it difficult to predict.

Trigger the buttons for every player which will require you to include a function. Stroll down to the very end of the program and write the below code:

def pressed(button):
print(str(button.pin.number) + " won the game")

Indentation is the tool Python uses to identify lines that are in your function. Thonny will indent the 2nd line automatically. Lastly, include the below line to discover which of the players is pushing the keys and do not forget that the lines must not be indented or else it will be treated as a function on Python.

right_button.when_pressed = pressed
left_button.when_pressed = pressed

Open your program and push one of the buttons immediately the LED is off. A message for the number one button to be pressed will be printed by Python shell at the down part of the Thonny window.

Message will pop up every time they press the button and a pin will be used for their names. Request for the names of the players, below the line from shuffled import uniform, write the below code:

left_name = input("Left player name is ") right_name = input("Right player name is ")
Go back to your function and replace the line print(str(button.pin.number) + " won the game") with:

if button.pin.number == 14:
print (left_name + " won the game")
else:
print(right_name + " won the game")

Tap the Run key and input the names of the players into the Python shell. When the button is pushed this time around, do it as fast as you can before the LED goes off, this will reveal the actual players' names and not pin numbers.

To amend the problem reported on the pressed buttons, you will introduce a new function from the **sys** that is 'system' library. Exit. Beneath the end of the import line, write the below code:

from os import _exit

At the last part of your function, below the line print(right_name + " won the game"), write the following:
_exit(0)

The indentation is very vital in this part: identify **_exit(0)** by four spaces and make it in line with **else:** let the **be 2** line at the top of it.

This will instruct the Python to put an end to the program after pressing the first key which means that the player with the secondary pressed button got nothing for losing the game.

Your final program should look like this:

```
from gpiozero import LED, Button
from time import sleep
from random import uniform
from os import _exit
left_name = input("Left player name is ")
right_name = input("Right player name is ")
led = LED(4)
right_button = Button(15)
left_button = Button(14)
led.on()
sleep(uniform(5, 10))
led.off()

def pressed(button):
    if button.pin.number == 14:
        print(left_name + " won the game")
    else:
        print(right_name + " won the game")
    _exit(0)

right_button.when_pressed = pressed
left_button.when_pressed = pressed
```

Tap the Run key and input the player names, hold on for the LED to go off to see the name of the winner. The two lines from Python will also be visible: when you see' Backend terminated (returncode: 0)' that is Python informing you that it got your _exit(0) command and exit the program.

The 'Start/Stop' is to restart the backend which means that the program is paused but not cancelled. To stop the program press the 'Stop' soft key.

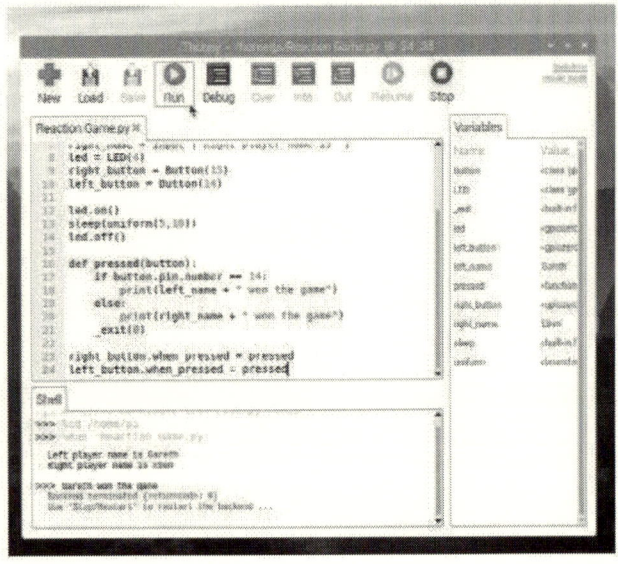

Quit the program when you have discovered the winner!

Hurray! You have successfully created your own physical game

CHALLENGE: IMPROVE THE GAME

Do you know how to address a loop for the game to keep running repeatedly?

Do not forget to clear the _exit(0) instruction!

How do you add a score counter to know who is winning even after multiples of rounds? Do you know you can set a timer to make you know the time it takes you to react to the light when going off?

Chapter 26: Physical Computing With Sense HAT

The Sense HAT, according to its application on the International Space Station, can be referred to as an add-on board for the Raspberry Pi which is equipped with sensors as well as an LED matrix display to perform varieties of functions.

Generally, the Raspberry Pi has been designed to support a special type of add-on board which is known as the Hardware Attached on Top (HAT). This add-on board is capable of getting hardware added such as microphones and lights, electronic relays and screens and even the Pi itself. The Sense HAT is however much more special type of the HAT genre.

The Sense HAT is popular for its use in a joint project called the Astro Pi space mission in which the Raspberry Pi foundation along with the UK space agency and European Space Agency collaborated.

They deployed Raspberry Pi boards along with Sense HATs, using the Astro Pi, into the international space station aboard a cargo rocket by Orbital Science Cygnus.

The Sense HATs was nicknamed Ed and Izzy by the astronauts. Astro Pi space mission saw the sense HAT successfully reaching the orbit high above the earth, giving this HAT the positive reputation of being now used to run code as well as carrying out the most scientific experiment by schoolchildren across Europe.

The Sense HAT hardware is available at all Raspberry Pi retailers and you can get it simulated in software as well if you don't want to buy one at present.

Introduction to the Sense HAT

The Sense HAT has a multi-functional add-on for the Raspberry Pi with amazing features. It designed with an 8x8 matrix of 64 red, green with blue LEDs which are all programmed and that can be controlled to produce colors from a range of millions. They are built with a five-way joystick controller as well as six-on-board sensors.

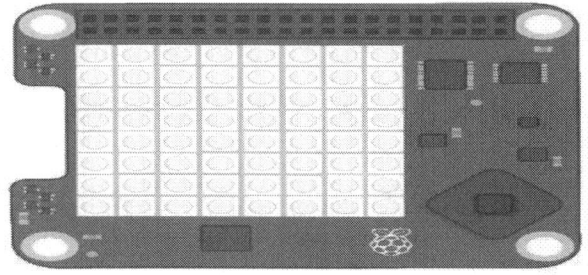

Gyroscope sensor: This is used in detecting any change in the angular velocity by keeping track of the gravity field of the earth. Talking of the gravity field, it's simply the force pulling things down towards the planet center. The gyroscopic sensor can tell you when the sense HAT rotates relatives to the Earth's surface as well as how fast it rotates.

Accelerometer: This measures acceleration force in multiple directions. The combined data from both gyroscope and accelerometer can be used detecting the direction which your Sensor HAT is pointing as well as how it is moved.

Magnetometer: This is used in measuring the magnetic field strength as well as keeping track of the movement of the Sense HAT. The magnetometer can also help in figuring out the direction of the magnetic north with the use of the earth's magnetic field of the earth. They can also be used in detecting metallic objects as well as electric fields.

All these three sensors that are, the gyroscope, accelerometer, and magnetometer are built into a single chip and they are labeled as ACCEL/GYRO/MAG on the circuit board of sense HAT.

Humidity sensor: This sensor measures the water vapor amount that is present in the air which is called the relative humidity. The relative humidity ranges from 0% to 100%. When at 0%, it means there is no presence of water at all in the air while 100% means that the air is completely saturated. We can easily predict if it's about the rain once we have information about the humidity.

Barometric pressure sensor: This measure the air pressure and it is also referred to as the barometer. It is a popular term when it comes to weather forecasting and can be used to track whether you are climbing up or down a mountain or hill as the air gets thinner or has a lower pressure compared to that of the sea level of the earth.

Temperature sensor: This measures the hotness or coldness of the surrounding environment and it is also being affected by how cold or hot the sense HAT is. It is to be noted that sensor HAT is not built with a separate temperature sensor but they simply rely on the temperature sensor that is available in the humidity or barometric pressure sensors. A program can be made to use one of these two sensors depending on what works for you.

Installation of the Sense HAT

Once you purchase your Sense HAT, you will need to get it unpacked to make sure you have every accessory completed packaged in it. It should be made up of the following:

- Sense HAT
- Spaces (which are the four metal or plastic pillars): This is used in stopping the Sense HAT from blending or flexing while the joystick is in use.
- Eight screws
- Metal pins in a black plastic strip similar to the GPIO pins on the Raspberry Pi; if this is available, get the strip pushed pin side up via the bottom of the Sense HAT until you hear the sound of a click.

Though the sense HAT will work without all these being installed they will help in protecting your Raspberry Pi, Sense HAT as well as The GPIO header from getting damaged.

WARNING

- Make sure the Raspberry Pi gets switched off and disconnected from its power supply before the

Hardware Attached on Top (HAT) modules is plugged in or removed from the GPIO header.

- When installing the HAT, make sure its lying flat before getting it installed and always check to make sure it is lined up with the GPIO header pins before getting it pushed down.
- Get the spacers installed by pushing the four screws up from the bottom of the Raspberry Pi via four mounting holes that are located at each corner and have the spacers twisted onto the screws. Get the sense HAT pushed down onto the GPIO header of the Raspberry Pi while ensuring that they are well lined up with the pins underneath and make sure it is flat as possible.
- Get the final four screws screwed via the sense HAT mounting holes into the spacers that were earlier installed. If properly installed, the sense HAT should be flat and leveled and it should not bend while pushing on its joystick.
- Have the power plug back into your Raspberry Pi. Once powered up the LEDs that are available on the Sense HAT will get lighted up with a rainbow

pattern after which you can switch off again. This signifies that the Sense HAT is now fully installed. '

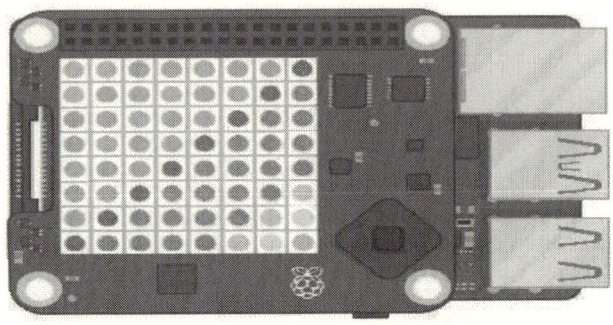

In case you want to detach the sense HAT again, undo the top screws and then lift the HAT off but make sure you do this carefully to avoid bending the pins that are available on the GPIO header due to the hard grip of the HAT. You can also employ the use of a small screwdriver. Then you can now remove the spacers from the Pi.

Hello, Sense HAT

Just like other programming projects, the sense HAT also has a beginning with a welcome message scrolling across the LED display. If you are making use of a sense HAT emulator, you can simply click on the Raspbian menu icon to get it loaded and then select the programming category and click on the Sense HAT emulator.

Chapter 27: Raspberry Pi 4 Projects— Creating a Portable Security Box on Raspberry Pi, 2, 3 and 4

Apart from creating a platform for beginners to begin coding, Raspberry serves as a foundation for more advanced programs and functions to thrive.

Some developers have been able to use Raspberry to create more impressive devices for use in our homes and workplaces. Some of these devices are quite complicated than others and as a result, requires more guidance to get it started and working, which is why this book has been written to enlighten beginners and users generally on projects to familiarize you with the optimal usage of this device.

Creating A Portable Security Box

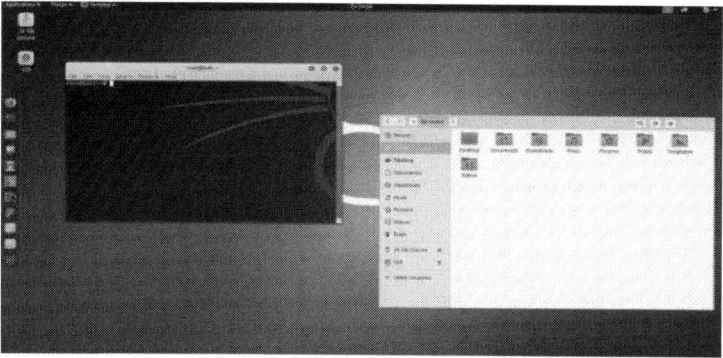

People that get paid to hack into security systems with the penetration testers, as well as other security personnel have been able to exploit the portability and accessibility of the Raspberry Pi 4 in carrying out their different functions. The fact that it is designed with a built-in Ethernet port, lesser power requirements and also can run any Linux software, makes it easy for integration with targeted networks.

Security operatives make use of software called Kali which is a Linux distro that is used for hacking tasks. The Raspberry Pi particularly has Kali software built purposely to be used with it and it's relatively easy to install.

The Kali Linux on the Raspberry Pi comes in handy for ethical hackers looking for more portability. Raspberry Pi 4 has been designed such that its usage requires less power including having a small size built. Its size can be compared as a credit card-sized computer such that when combined with Kali Linux, you will derive a super-portable network testing machine that can be carried anywhere.

It can be used on a laptop in cracking nearby Wi-Fi passwords, testing for Bluetooth vulnerabilities, spoof networks, and many other things.

If you want to avoid the installation of Kali Linux on your primary computer, you can simply have a touch screen added.

Requirements Needed To Install the Kali Linux

To get the installation of the Kali Linux started, you will need the following:

- Raspberry Pi 2, 3, or 4
- Power supply
- HDMI cable
- A minimum of 8GB SD-Card
- Keyboard
- Mouse

Go to the Offensive Security download area, search and download Kali Linux 2.0 image file for Raspberry Pi. It is to be noted that there are other image files available so you will need to scroll down to find the Raspberry Pi 2/3 download. Make sure you verify that you are installing the genuine Kali version in a situation where you are using Kali for security testing.

Once the download is completed, you will then need to get the file extracted. But if your computer does not have the right software to get the file extracted, download WinRAR and get it installed for the extraction of the image file. Once extraction has been completed, it is then ready to be written on an SD-Card whose minimum size should be 8GB.

Nevertheless, it is advisable to use a card which is up to 16GB or 32GB because it gives room for more space to have tools and apps downloaded and run.

The next step is to have the image file loaded into Win32 Disk Imager and have it written to the correct drive and ensure that you have picked the correct one because it will overwrite any drive selected.

It is to be noted that a few minutes will be required to write the package and once it is done, you will be prompted with a message which states "Write Successful." And in case you don't know, the Win32DiskImager is a Window program used for saving and restoring images from removable drives.

The Installation of Kali on Raspberry Pi

Kali will be ready for installation on the Raspberry Pi once the image has been written to the SD-Card.

All the needed accessories can now be connected such as making use of the HDMI cable in plugging the TV or monitor as well as the addition of the keyboard and mouse for control.

Power up the Pi which will result in the bootup process causing the screen to go blank a few times before boot up is done.

You will be prompted by a login page where you will need to enter your username and password. By default, the username and password are root and or respectively.

It is, however, advisable to change your login credentials into something that guarantees more security, but you will also need to change the SSH host keys because the Kali image for the Raspberry Pi 4 also comes with a set of pre-configured default keys. To change the SSH host keys, you can employ the use of the commands below:

- root@kali:~ rm /etc/ssh/ssh_host_*
- root@kali:~ dpkg-reconfigure openssh-server

- root@kali:~ service ssh restart

Installation of Hacking Tools

Once you have been able to effectively install the Kali Linux following all the instructions stated above, input the command startx from the command line to make it boot into the graphical desktop environment. The ARM-based Kali images come with a bare minimum of tools that are pre-installed by default.

Nevertheless, to get new ones installed, you can make use of the Kali metapackages. There is the availability of various metapackages that contains different groups of tools to be used for specific purposes such as Wi-Fi analysis or password cracking.

To have access to the full list of metapackages that are available as well as all the tools that are included with the default desktop image of Kali, install the "kali-linux-full." You can also get each available tool with the "kali-linux-all" metapackage.

Depending on your needs, you can also decide to pick specific metapackages. It is to be noted that all metapackages are installed with the use of standard Linux apt-get method.

For instance, to have access to the complete toolset, you can make use of the command apt-get install kali-linux-all. After the installation of your preferred tools with the default passwords changed, your Kali will be ready for use.

After the full installation of Kali, apart from its usefulness in security operations, it is also useful for playing around with new tools without posing any risk of damage to your primary machine, though you should ensure that you are only hacking targets that have given you express permission.

Chapter 28: Raspberry Pi 4 Projects—Setting up Raspberry Pi as a VPN Server

The function of the VPN is to help you in making your online identity to protect your activity from being tracked while browsing the internet or doing other things like engaging in conversations. VPNs are famous for their use in our regular computers and it is used in a similar way when it comes to our micro-computer such as the Raspberry Pi. Examples of VPN services that can be used with the Raspberry Pi are Express VPN, IPVanish, HideMy Ass as well as the SaferVPN.

Fortunately, the Raspberry Pi can also be used as a VPN server as well by using it in the creation of a personal VPN hotspot for protecting your identity information from being leaked to any website that is opened via your network.

Install a client on the Raspberry Pi and get connected with the use of your router and your identity will get scrambled before it hits the external network.

Set your Raspberry Pi up as a VPN server by taking the following steps:

i. Install Raspbian to gain access to the command line.

ii. Install the VPN client to protect your identity by making use of the PiVPN script. You are recommended to make use of the OpenVPN as your VPN client.

A secured, as well as an encrypted connection, can be created for your home network anywhere in the world by plugging in a VPN server into your router. There are several advantages attached to this, such as:

- Easy access to files on your NAS without endless configurations or while the connection is being encrypted.
- You will also get an option to make use of your laptop on a public Wi-Fi hotspot without the risk of any intruder accessing your transmitted data.
- It also gives you complete control over your data having a rest of mind that all your data is safe.
- No special hardware is needed to get your VPN working as well.

Installation of the VPN Servers

- For this guide, we will be using the PiVPN OpenVPN installer that is not compatible with the latest Raspbian stretch distro. Therefore, we will be focusing on the use of the previous version called Raspbian Jesse.
- The Jessie was the most popularly used till July 2017 but the PiVPN script is presently been updated to support Raspbian stretch for its use.
- It is advisable to make use of the Raspbian Lite version because it will be used on the Raspberry Pi

in the command-line mode. The Lite version does not come with a graphical user interface.

- Get on your browser to get the 2017 file of raspbian-jessie-lite.zip file and get the .img file in it extracted.

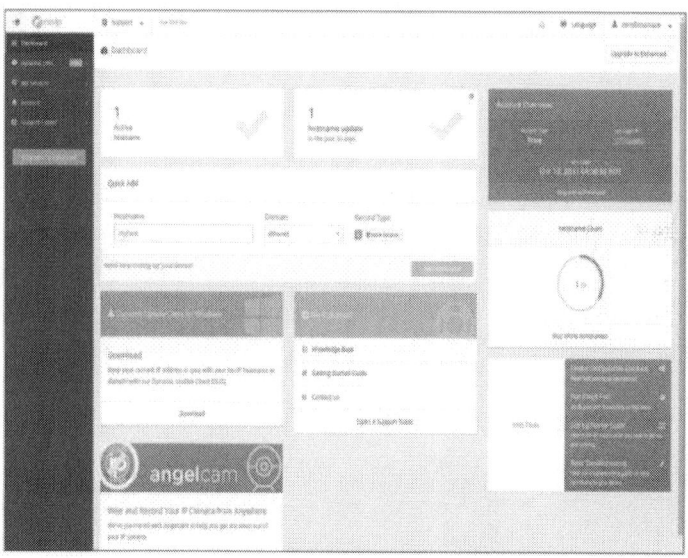

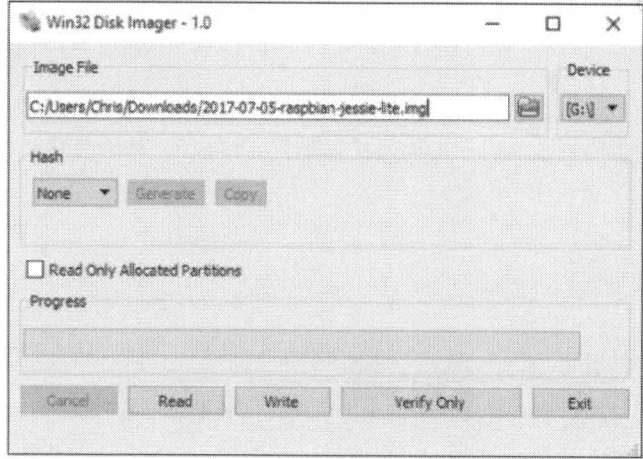

- Download and install the Win32 Disk Imager.
- Get your microSD card plugged into your card reader and ensure that there is nothing you still need on the card.
- Run the Win32 Disk Imager.
- You will be required to input in your administrator password if you are logged in using the standard Windows account.
- Go to the top at the right side of the white box and click on the blue folder icon.
- Go to Raspbian Jessie Lite .img file that you extracted and double click on it.
- It is, however, important to note that the file browser might default to the download folder of the administrator account instead of the current user. It is therefore important to manually browse for the right location.
- You will also need to check your microSD card is the right one listed under Device and select Write.
- Eject the microSD card once the process done and put it in the Raspberry Pi and boot up.

- You will require a keyboard and monitor to be connected to your Raspberry Pi through the internet will not be required yet.
- Make use of the normal login to gain access by making use of the username: pi; password: raspberry.
- You can hide the Raspberry Pi in the corner that is next to your router since it is just going to be used as a server. It is advisable to set up your Pi to be controlled remotely in the crustless mode.
- You will need to enable Secure Shell (SSH) by typing in the command sudo raspi-config to control in the crustless mode.

Once set up, you should change the password immediately to give you the sole access to the SSH, by taking the following steps:

- Select Option 1 and input in your password twice to alter it.
- Go to option 5 which is the interfacing options.
- Select P2 SSH.

- You will be prompted with a question saying "Would you like the SSH server to be enabled?" answer yes to this question.
- Once you select YES, Pi will confirm that your SSH is on and select Finish afterward.
- Type in the command sudo shutdown now, to get your Raspberry Pi shut down.
- Get your keyboard and monitor unplugged and get the Raspberry Pi plugged into your router using the Ethernet cable.

Now you will be able to control your Raspberry Pi remotely without the use of the keyboard and monitor.

How to find your Raspberry Pi

- You will be required to turn your Raspberry Pi on again after which you will need to give it a few seconds to boot up. After which you can now find the Raspberry Pi on your network.
- Make use of the Find Android app which lists every device that is connected to your network and it is to be noted that the Raspberry will be shown as Raspberry on the list including the IP address.

- Go to Windows and make use of the IP scanner like the Angry IP scanner for example. The Angry IP scanner gets your Raspberry Pi listed as raspberry pi.local located in the Hostname column.

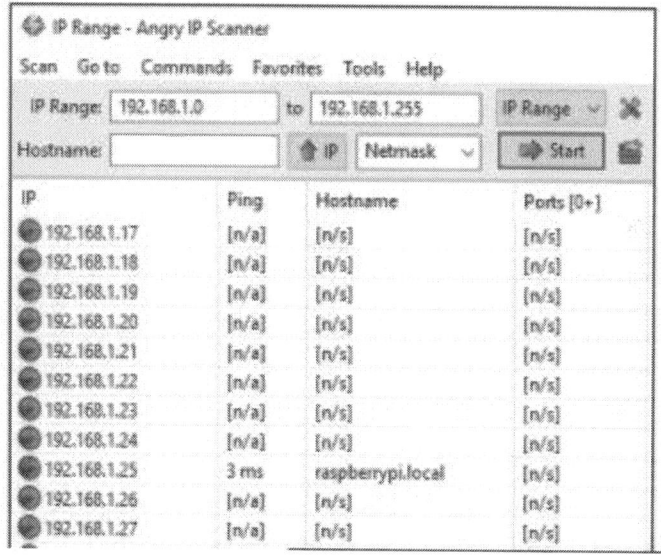

- You will need to download and install the PuTTY SSH client to get your Raspberry Pi connected.
- After this place, the IP address of your Raspberry Pi in the Hostname box while you check to be sure you're SSH radio button is selected and finally selects Open.
- You will be prompted with a security message. Check again to be sure the IP address of your

Raspberry Pi is the one you have at the top-left of the PuTTY window and finally select YES to confirm that you trust the device.

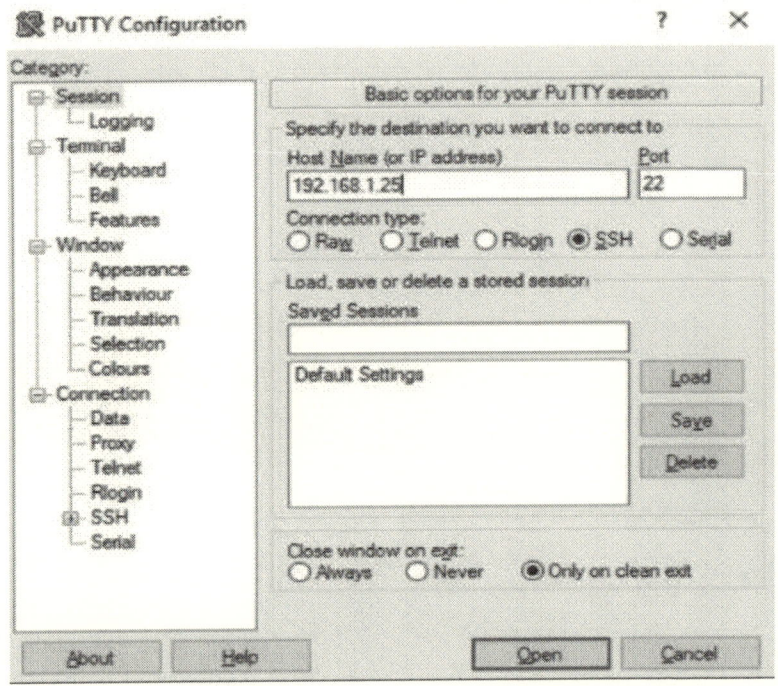

Now you will have access to log in using the username and password of your Raspberry Pi including a command-line used similarly to having the physical presence of your Raspberry Pi. You should have the Linux updates downloaded and installed by making use of the command sudo apt-get update and sudo apt-get upgrade afterward.

Then you can now install the OpenVPN through the PiVPN installer by taking the following steps:

i. Type curl –L https://install.pivpn.io | bash to get the installer started.

ii. Navigate to the installer by making use of the arrow keys of the keyboard.

iii. Press the tab as well as the shift-tab in switching to the YES/NO including the OK/Cancel option located at the bottom of the different pages and back again. It is to be noted that you might also need the use of a space bar in selecting some options as well.

Static IP

You will need to set up a static IP address to notify your router about the location of your Raspberry Pi on your network so that this can be forwarded to incoming VPN traffic. It is acceptable to keep using the IP address that is currently being used by your Raspberry Pi but it is to be noted that your router might not assign the same IP address to a different device that is under your network automatically.

To carry this out, if asked about using your current network settings as your static address, you can click on NO and change the last number of the address afterward. For example with an IP address of 192.168.1.100, you can get the 100 which is the last number here changed. To ensure an address hasn't been taken yet, you can make use of the Angry IP scanner or Fing.

The IPv4 default gateways should already be set on the IP address of your router and as a result, it will need no adjustment. You can just do a proper check to ensure the settings are correct and then select YES to continue.

You will need to follow the steps to choose which user's directory will be needed to store the configurations of your OpenVPN:

i. The default "pi" will be the only one installed, so you will have no other choice than to have it selected.

ii. You will be prompted by a piece of advice from the next screen to enable unattended-upgrades for the Raspberry Pi to get itself automatically updated using security patches.

The security patches are very useful for a machine which is always connected to the internet having its network port opened all the time.

iii. To enable the feature in the last step, select YES.

iv. You can now choose between using the TCP or the UDP protocols. It is more preferable to make use of the UDP because they are faster through the TCP also comes in handy in certain situations.

v. Select "UDP" and click on the OK option.

vi. Let the port remains as the default (1194) and selects the OK option. It is important to have the port number noted somewhere and ensure the port is correctly displayed on the screen.

Paranoia Level

- It is to be noted that you will be prompted with three levels of encryption.
- For the PiVPN installer, you are recommended to choose the 2,048-bit encryption which is regarded as a good compromise considering security issues and the time taken for the key to be generated.

- For security, 4,096 come in handy and you will also be given the option to download key components from public key generation service for generation time to be reduced.
- If the security is an important factor for you which is otherwise referred to as the paranoid in terms of the PiVPN installer, you can get your keys generated from the scratch. You can get this done on the Raspberry Pi 3 in less than an hour.
- However, it is important to note that the PiVPN installer does not give room for going back to alter a setting that has already being made. Once you have a setting such as the IP address wrong, you will need to quit the installer again and then restart and this will also involve you spending an extra hour on generating of keys.

Getting Connected To Pi

- Apart from now having the keys for the encryption of your connection, you should also understand how users can get to connect to your Raspberry Pi. Connection can be established for users in two ways:

- The use of your external IP address.
- The use of dynamic DNS service.
- Making use of the external IP service is easier because of its less involvement of your router but for its downside, its IP address is not constant on most of the residential broadband packages which could make connecting to your VPN quite difficult when you are not indoor.
- The dynamic DNS service will be useful for avoiding the periodical change in IP address by giving you an address such as pivpn.dynamicdns.com which will automatically translate to the current external IP address of your router.
- Once you enter the details into the settings of your router, the DNS service will automatically get updated by the router as soon as the external IP address changes. This ensures that the address that was chosen by you always translates into your home connection's external address.
- You will need to find out the dynamic DNS services that are supported by the router by going into the settings menu on the router. To access this, you will need to sign up on the dynamic DNS service web

page and in case of some routers like the Netgear D700; you can sign up directly from the interface.

- In a situation where your router does not support dynamic DNS, you can sign up for a No-IP account to compensate for this by making use of the Windows application. This will automatically send your external IP address to No-IP and for this to work; you must make sure your computer is on.

- After you have completed the signup, you will be given an option of selecting a hostname with different domains and it will automatically fill in your IP address. In a situation where your hostname has already been taken, you will need to keep trying different hostname or domain combinations until you stumble on an available one.

- Then you should have your hostname listed at the Hostname section of the No-IP dashboard with the No Dynamic Update Detected underneath. Select this option and you will be enlightened by the wizard as regards setting up your DNS getting updated on your router.

- Go to the PiVPN installer and select the Public IP or an external IP address or choose the DNS entry if you are making use of the dynamic DNS. In the case you chose the DNS entry, you will be required to put in your dynamic DNS Hostname and check properly to be sure it is right before confirmation.

- For users connecting to your VPN, you will need to be requested for the DNS Provider because it will be needed in browsing the web through a VPN server of the Raspberry Pi. The DNS server can view whatever websites that must have been visited by those connecting to your VPN as a result, you are advised to build your DNS server if you need some privacy.
- At the final stage, you will be required to "run pivpn add to create the ovpn profiles," however you will need to have your Raspberry Pi rebooted first.
- Select the OK option to start rebooting.
- Forward the necessary port available on your router.
- Go to the settings of the router and get a port forwarded to your Raspberry Pi to notify your router where it will be sending the incoming VPN connections irrespective if you decide to use an external IP address is connecting to your Raspberry Pi VPN or using the dynamic DNS.

- You should visit the portforward.com for a comprehensive router list. Stick to the use of the default OpenVPN UDP port 1194.

- Ensure it is added to the IP address of your Raspberry Pi while ensuring the UDP is selected and not the TCP.

Access Granted

- Get logged back into your Raspberry Pi making use of PuTTY.
- To ensure your Raspberry Pi is updated with the latest security patches required, type the commands: sudo-apt get update then sudo apt-get upgrade.
- For the users or clients that will be connecting to your VPN, you will need to have their OpenVPN profiles added.
- There will be a username and password allocated to each user which will need to be used along with a special file that was generated by you with the use of PiVPN to get connected.
- To give a user or client access to your VPN, you will need to type pivpn add and input in the username

and password for such a client. Once this is done, the .ovpn file will be generated and will be automatically copied to /home/pi/ovpns. Any other profiles that you intend adding can also be added. To get profile removed type in pivpn revoke followed by the profile name.

- Making use of the SFTP is the easiest way to copy the .ovpn files off the Raspberry Pi. To do this, you will need an FTP client or WinSCP.
- You will need to download and install the WinSCP and when you run it, a screen will be displayed where you should ensure selecting the SFTP under the File protocol.
- Go to the Hostname and enter the IP address of your Raspberry Pi ensuring the port number is 22 and input in your username as well as password. Select Login after inputting the required details. Select YES to add the Host key of Raspberry Pi added to the cache and avoid getting this warning again.
- You will be navigated to /home/pi by default; therefore you will need to browse the ovpns folder

after which you should get the .ovpn copied to your PC.

- To get connected to your VPN, you will need the combination of the .ovpn file along with the correct username and password. It is to be noted that the client software will be needed for this.
- The next step is to download and install the OpenVPN Installer.
- The copy your .ovpn files to C:\Program Files\OpenVPN\config. In a situation where you intend sending these files to other people, it will be a good idea to encrypt the files using the 7-Zip first to have them secured. It is, however, important to note that most email services will not allow you to get an encrypted file sent over them as an attachment so they will need to be hosted in a file sharing service like the Dropbox. After which you can send a link to the Dropbox folder which contains the encrypted file.
- It is also advisable to get the username including the password sent separately from the 7-Zip encrypted .ovpn file. You can preferably make use of an encrypted platform like the WhatsApp.

- To get the OpenVPN Gui loaded. Go to the System Tray and right-click it. You will then be prompted with a list of OpenVPN profiles that have been installed.
- Click on connect afterward for a secure connection to your Raspberry Pi.
- Connect using a smartphone running in the wireless hotspot mode is the easiest way to check if your VPN is working from outside a home network.

Chapter 29: Installing Full Windows 10 on Raspberry Pi 3 And 4

The Operating system of Microsoft can be installed on the Raspberry Pi 3 Model B or B+ boards by making use of windows on ARM installer (WoA) which is available on the GitHub. The operating system previously used on the Raspberry Pi devices is the Windows IoT core operating systems but there is now an opportunity to have the full Windows 10 OS installed.

The Windows on Arm installer is available on the GitHub and do require bundled binaries and WoA core package for use.

To install the full windows 10 on your Raspberry Pi 3, you will require the following:

- A set of binaries and software which are all available on the GitHub page.
- A Raspberry Pi 3B or B+
- A Windows 10 ARM64 image which can also be found linked on the GitHub page.
- MicroSD card having at least 16GB storage space with an A1 rating.

Running Windows 10 IoT Core on Raspberry Pi

If you want to have the full version of the Windows including the Windows 10 IoT core running on your Raspberry, you can have a stripped version of the operating system up and running on the microcomputer.

In the case of the Raspberry Pi Model B+, they don't have the required processing power to give room for the running of the Windows 10 full version on them. They only have the 1GB RAM as well as a 1.4GHz ARM-based processor.

It is advisable to go for the Windows 10 IoT Core which is a basic version of the operating system of Microsoft and it also has an added advantage of being functional on less powerful platforms. It gives you room to run a single UWP app at a time because of its lightweight properties. A license is not needed except you are commercializing your creations and you will need a limited amount of equipment.

First, you will need the Raspberry Pi 3, spare microSD card including a separate Windows computer that has a microSD card reader. Other tools that will be needed include a text editor, Visual studio, the SDKs add-ons including certificates.

The next thing is to set up the memory card for the Raspberry Pi which you will be using.

Make use of the New Out Of Box Software (NOOBS) installer to make installation easier.

Get a bootable card created from a Windows PC or Laptop afterward with the use of the IoT dashboard app of Microsoft.

Make use of the Broadcom Raspberry Pi 2 & 3 or 4 option as well as the OS build or Windows 10 IoT Core in setting up your device.

Specify a password and choose a Wi-Fi network.

Install the operating system on the Raspberry Pi-compatible memory card.

Get the card inserted into the Raspberry Pi. Once inserted, your device should be ready to get booted up with the latest version of the Windows IoT Core.

Installing Windows 10 Iot Core on Raspberry Pi

Windows is constantly evolving its platforms and they are not only focusing on the apps including their flashy graphics, but they have also been able to extend their evolutions to other and new platforms as well. With the diminishing reign of the Windows phone as well as the Windows 10 Mobile, this has allowed Microsoft to focus more on their major products, improving more on the desktop edition as well as giving room for new hardware in more intelligent manners. Now considering the Raspberry Pi which is not just a conventional workstation with it's Pi 3 Model B+ having just 1GB of RAM with 1.4GHz ARM-based processor, will not be enough to run the full version of the Windows 10. Windows have been able to improve in this area by coming up with the Windows 10 IoT Core to get installed instead due to its lightweight properties.

It is to be noted that the IoT core has a very limited experience in which you can run on a single UWP app at a time and it shouldn't be seen as a desktop replacement. Its basic installation has been made free and it's a very interesting app to try out, all you will need is to make payment for the license in case you have a plan to get the results distributed.

If you want to explore the app development world as well as making much more optimal use of your Raspberry Pi, having a good understanding of setting up the IoT development platform. It is known for its low cost and consumes lesser power as well. You will need the following to integrate the IoT core:

- Raspberry Pi 3
- A spare microSD card
- Windows computer has a microSD card reader for the installation media to be created

- Download Visual studio, text editor including certificates, when you are ready to start with the development of the applications.

Preparation of your Raspberry Pi for IoT Core

The Windows 10 IoT Core has been made available for different lightweight system on a chip device with the ARM-based Raspberry Pi as well as DragonBoard platforms. They have also been designed to run on Intel-powered MinnowBoard.

In terms of cost and ease of use, the Pi comes in handy and in a situation where you like to switch to other projects, Pi is much more flexible supporting a range of both hardware add-ons including applications.

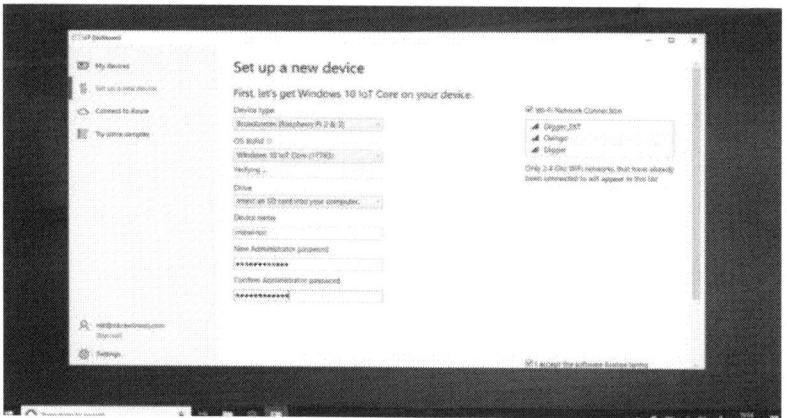

In getting your Pi ready, you will need to set up your microSD for the model of your Raspberry Pi. It is to be noted that the Pi board doesn't have a built-in BIOS as you might think and the required code is read directly from the microSD.

This is the reason cards can't be switched directly between Pi's different model even between closest of all the models, the Pi 3 with the Pi 3 Model B+. You can now easily set up the default Raspbian OS and for the Windows 10 IoT core using the New Out Of Box Software (NOOBS).

You can also make use of Microsoft's IoT dashboard app in creating a bootable card with the use of a Windows PC or laptop.

To download, click on the tab that reads "Download the Windows 10 IoT Core Dashboard"

When asked if you want to run or save it, select Run.

You will be prompted with a request, select Yes to allow it to make changes to your PC.

The IoT Dashboard

- When the Windows 10 IoT dashboard opens, it shows a list of "My devices" which will be empty by default.
- As soon as your Windows 10 IoT core starts running on your Pi, it will enable you to get access to the features remotely.
- Go to the sidebar and select "Set up a new device."
- Sign in using your Microsoft account if you are not logged in already. You will be prompted with a set of options as shown below.

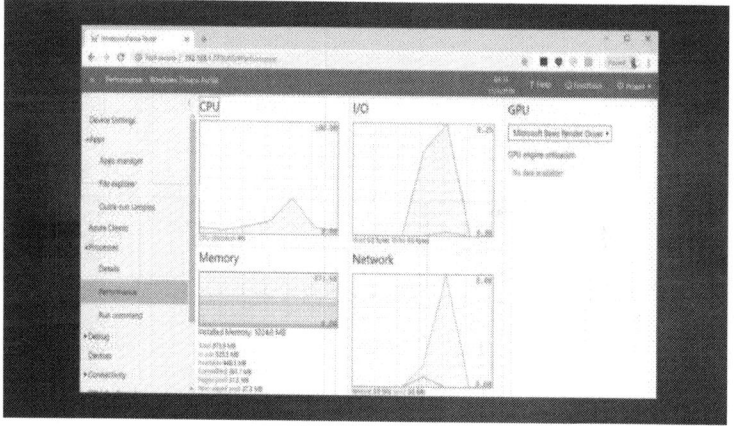

- The next step is to set your device to Broadcomm Raspberry Pi 2 & 3 or 4
- Select your OS to build which should be Windows 10 IoT core. It is advisable to go for the latest version which is 17763 at the time of writing this book.

- Specify a device name as well as the password. The default name is minwinpc which is quite easy to remember and you are advised to use a good password and avoid using the same password you used for the login for other services.
- Go to the right-hand side of the window where you will find a list of Wi-Fi network connections. Select your preferred network on the list and it is to be noted your Raspberry Pi will automatically get online at boot up.
- In case there is a change of location and need to boot up your Windows 10 IoT core in a different location, there will always be a chance to choose an SSID and provide it with the passphrase.
- Insert the SD card into your PC once this is done. It is to be noted that the Raspberry Pi makes use of MicroSD card while most laptops make use of only a full-sized SD card slot.
- Therefore, it is advisable to purchase a cheaper microSD adapter and make sure you have anything that might be available on your microSD card backed up in case you need to keep the files because

once the setup process is complete, all files will be completely wiped out.

- Due to the same reason, once your card has been inserted, make sure you properly check to make sure it has been correctly selected by the IoT dashboard as the installation destination. Both the name and capacity should be shown as expected and to be sure of this, double click on the dropdown menu and get all the options reviewed to select the correct one.

- Accept the terms of the software license by ticking the box and then select the Download and install option afterward to get the process completed. The latest build for your device will get downloaded by the IoT dashboard. It is to be noted that this file is large and as a result, it might take up to an hour to download using home broadband.

- The image will be stored locally afterward and you won't have to get it downloaded again in case you want to flash the microSD in the future.

After installation is complete, you might be faced with situations where you will be prompted with the Dashboard needing to format a different drive for it to be readable. Once faced with this, take the following steps:

i. Cancel the message.

ii. Eject the SD card.

iii. Insert the SD card into your Raspberry Pi.

iv. Switch on the Power to boot into the Windows 10 IoT core.

Booting into the IoT core

- Booting into the IoT core might take a little longer showing the Windows logo or a blank screen at first time booting.
- You will be asked to choose a Wi-Fi network that can be skipped if you already chose a network during the image creation.
- The next page after this will be the device overview. The brief rundown about the spec of your hardware will contain the IP address including other information as shown below:

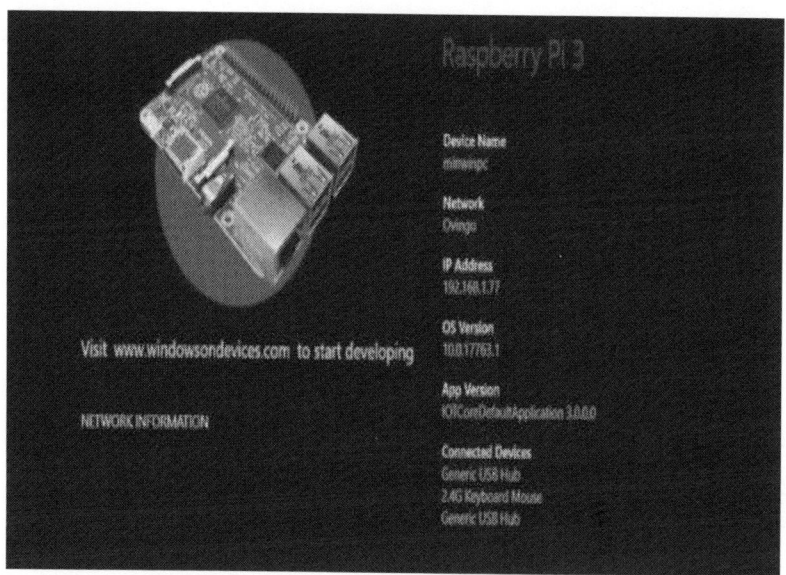

- Once you are booted into the Operating system, it is advisable to check for any available updates.
- Go to the sidebar and click on the icon denoted by a red person to get logged in to your Microsoft account.
- Open the Settings by clicking on the cog icon.
- Select App Updates fin the sidebar.
- Apart from the ability to use the Raspberry Pi as a regular desktop PC, it can also be used for headless operation due to its compact and low-power design even with the exclusion of the monitor, mouse or keyboard.

- Microsoft has also built the device such that it now has a remote access feature in its IoT dashboard. To make use of this functionality:
- Return to your personal computer.
- Go to the IoT dashboard sidebar and select "My Devices."
- Right-click on your Raspberry Pi and click on Open in the Device Portal which will result in the opening of your default browser which contains different details about your IoT Core System.
- Use "Administrator" as the username while your password should be the one you specified during the setup process. In a situation where no password was entered, make use of the default password which is "p@ssword"

In a situation where your Pi is not displayed under My devices pane, check to make sure your connection is not blocked by Windows. When this happens, you can do the following:

- Search for "Allow an app through Windows Firewall" in the start menu.
- Go to the firewall control panel.

- Scroll down the list of applications and ensure that the WINDOWS10IOTCOREDASHBOARD.EXE is selected for easy access to private networks.
- The device portal enables you to perform a different kind of management tasks which includes:
- Changing your password.
- Setting the remote device time.
- Monitoring the performance and resource usage of your Raspberry Pi.
- With the device portal, you can also get the application deployed to the device.

How to get an application deployed to the device

i. Go to the sidebar and expand the Apps section.

ii. Click on the Apps manager option.

iii. To get a package uploaded from your desktop, select "Choose file"

How to Run the Powershell Remotely

- You can remotely access the file system of Pi and run commands on it directly by going through the dashboard. Do this by following the instructions below:

- Go to the IoT Dashboard's My Devices and right-click its entry.
- Select Launch PowerShell.
- Confirm that Windows can have changes made to your PC.
- Input your login details which should navigate you to the PowerShell prompt. This works similarly as if you are typing directly into your Raspberry Pi.

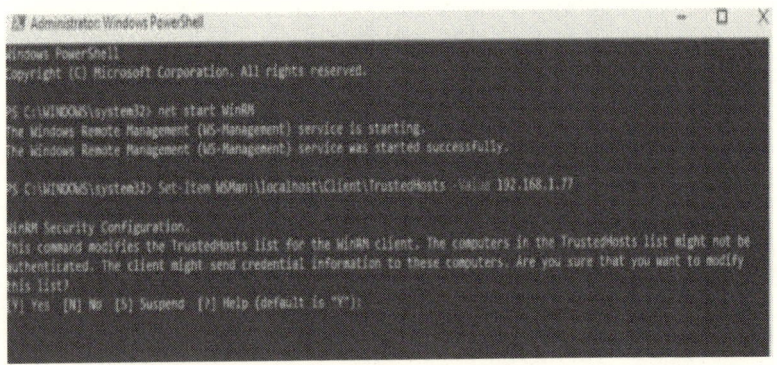

If you have a problem initiating a connection, check to be sure the format of credentials is correct. The format should be in the form: username prefixed by the IP address of the Pi as well as a backslash for example here, we have 192.168.1.77\Administrator.

If this doesn't work, then probably your Pi is not included in the list of trusted devices. Then you will have to:

i. Quit the remote PowerShell session to get this fixed.

ii. Go to the windows search box where you are required to type in PowerShell.

iii. Right-click on the search result and click on "Run as Administrator."

Input in "new start WinRM" and select return to ensure that your Windows Remote Management is working fine.

Type in "Set-Item WSMAN:\localhost\Client\TrustedHosts -Value 192.168.1.77" to replace "192.168.1.77" using the address that was copied down from the screen of your device overview.

Then your PowerShell session will be ready for launching on your Pi and it is known to be very interactive as well.

Deploying your IoT applications

- It should be noted that IoT applications are not installed in the same way as the normal Windows apps and there is no SETUP.EXE file that can be double-clicked on and most times, the target systems won't have a mouse and monitor included.

- If an application is developed using the IoT Core, you will need to get it packaged into an image that can be booted. It should also contain both your code as well as the required operating system with device driver files which can be flashed onto the microSD for proper distribution.

- The card is designed to start up an IoT – ready device like the Raspberry Pi or the Arduino board and it can also be used in launching a single application that can be machine controller, time-lapse camera, voice assistant, etc.

- It is to be noted that if you are a fan of the IoT development, the IoT Core distribution being described in this book can only be used in creating test images which are a major target for developers that have an interest in prototyping new designs.

- There also retail images that are compiled to be used by consumers and they can be used on corporate networks as well. They can also be effective secured to protect it from intruders. A core pro license can also be used in generating them but this doesn't leave out all the testing and development that is required on a normal IoT Core system and they can upgrade when it's time for your final media to be built.

Chapter 30: Troubleshooting 7 Tips

ISSUE: Plugged my Raspberry Pi in, but nothing is displayed on the screen

- If this happens, check to make sure you connected your cables in the right order.
- Make sure your HDMI cable is plugged in before the power.
- Lastly, make sure you turned on your screen and the correct input is selected before plugging in your Raspberry Pi's power.

ISSUE: The red light on my Pi is the only light turned on, is it broken?

When power is supplied to your Raspberry Pi, both the red and green light should come on by default the software activity is indicated by the green light with a flash. Once you detect the absence of an activity, then there is probably a problem with your microSD card. You can then go ahead to check the following.

- Make sure the microSD card is correctly inserted into your Raspberry Pi.
- Make sure that your microSD card contains the software needed by the Raspberry.

ISSUE: Is another computer needed to use a Raspberry Pi?

Another computer is not needed to use your Raspberry Pi because it's a computer itself. But in a situation where you need to get a new MicroSD card created, there will be a need for occasional access to a different computer.

ISSUE: Already copied NOOBS to an SD card, but it's getting stuck on the splash screen, what can I do?

- When this happens, check if the microSD card is corrupt.
- If corrupt, try a different card but if not and the NOOBS doesn't still work, then try installing Raspbian directly.

ISSUE: My keyboard keeps outputting the wrong characters

- The Raspbian and NOOBS will default to the UK keyboard settings when in use.
- Nevertheless, you were given the chance to change the location settings at the first start-up of the Raspbian using the raspi-config menu.
- Open a terminal window to get the menu back in Raspbian OS and type in sudo raspi-config.

- Select the "Internationalization menu"
- Select the "keyboard setup menu"
- In a situation where your exact keyboard does not appear on the list, select one of the generic 102, 103, or 104 keyboards.
- Choose the US, if you get the US keyboard.
- Note that the default keyboard layout is the English UK.
- There will be a need for you to scroll down and select the other so as to get back to the Country of origin menu.
- Select English US from the country of origin menu.
- Scroll to the top of the list and click on English US from the menu of the keyboard layout.
- Finish up the other menus
- Reboot.

A note from the Author

Thanks for reading through this guide. We do hope you find this guide useful and informative. If you do, please leave a review on Amazon.

Best Wishes

Sam O. Collins

Made in the
USA
Middletown, DE